The Great Baltimore Fire

The Great Baltimore Fire

Peter B. Petersen

Maryland Historical Society

BALTIMORE

Copyright © 2004 by
The Press at the Maryland Historical Society

Printed in Canada

The Press at the Maryland Historical Society
201 W. Monument Street
Baltimore, Maryland 21201

DESIGNED BY JAMES F. BRISSON

Library of Congress cataloging-in-publication data
Petersen, Peter B., 1932–
    The great Baltimore fire / Peter B. Petersen.
        p. cm.
    Includes bibliographical references (p.) and index.
    ISBN 0-938420-92-5 (alk. paper)
    1. Baltimore (Md.)—History—20th century 2.
Fires—Maryland—Baltimore—History—20th century. I. Title.

F189.B157P48 2004
975.2'6043—dc22

2003068601

To my loving wife Jan on our 48th anniversary,

our three sons John, Bill, and Jim,

their wives Charlotte, Melissa, and Amy,

their children John & Ellie; Matthew, Will & Jack;

and Katie, Julie, & Eric, and to our 15–20 great-grandchildren

who will extend our love into the 22nd century

❧ Contents ❧

29 – 31

⋙ Acknowledgments ⋘

WHILE ATTENDING MY FIRST Academy of Management meeting more than two decades ago, I became hooked on studying the subject of leadership and management. As a new professor of management at Johns Hopkins, I wanted to concentrate on incidents and examples that were relevant to my interests, and hearing about the actions of leaders of business and industry during the early years of the twentieth century captured my attention. Discussions about attempts to apply scientific management, given by management history scholars such as Daniel A. Wren, Ronald G. Greenwood, Charles D. Wrege, Alfred A. Bolton, and Richard Hodgetts, held particular appeal.

Searching for historical examples of scientific management in Baltimore, I found that Frederick W. Taylor, Henry L. Gantt, and especially Taylor's youngest follower, Morris L. Cooke, had worked closely with Edward B. Passano, president of the printing firm of Williams and Wilkins, later the Waverly Press. Fortunately, Johns Hopkins' late dean emeritus of engineering, Robert H. Roy, also had worked with Passano during the 1920s, 1930s, and early 1940s and had heard him tell of the failed attempt to apply scientific management principles at this highly successful firm. Ironically, a more interesting—indeed, thrilling—tale Rob Roy told concerned the quick thinking, hard work, and resourcefulness of Ned Passano during the Great Baltimore Fire of 1904. Having worked with Passano for nineteen years, Dean Roy had listened on many occasions to Passano's stories about his company's difficult but triumphant recovery from that disaster.

My informal discussions with Rob Roy, as well as my interview with him on February 28, 1984, that led to a thirty-three-page transcript, sparked my interest in examining the Great Baltimore Fire from the perspective of crisis management. My focus was on how various leaders acted during this crisis and the results of their actions. In addition to my discussions with Rob Roy, I had the good fortune of becoming acquainted with E. Magruder (Mac) Passano, Jr., the grandson of Ned Passano. Mac was extremely helpful and supportive of my research, providing sound counsel and a wealth of information from the files on the early operations of the company. Indeed, my heartfelt thanks extend to all of those who years ago pointed me in the direction of the story about Baltimore's great fire.

The collection of background research

ACKNOWLEDGMENTS

material on the Great Baltimore Fire initially proved slow, but it promptly became more promising with the assistance and advice of Jeannie Stinchcomb at the Enoch Pratt Free Library. She suggested that I concentrate on their Maryland Room, where I spent many worthwhile hours gathering information. Reference Librarian Lee Lears, my first contact in the Maryland Room, introduced me to Jeff Korman, manager of the Maryland Department. Korman's knowledge of the Maryland Room's holdings saved me countless hours, and his advice on searching for additional information led to further findings. Don Bonsteel and Eva Slezak provided valuable help as I plowed through stacks of archival material. In the final weeks of completing the manuscript, Nancy Derevjanik, part-time librarian, and Layne L. Bosserman, author's assistant, were very helpful. I am indebted to the staff of the Pratt Library for their friendly support and the material they provided.

Appreciation also is due to Dr. Vincent Fitzpatrick, curator of the Mencken Collection at the Pratt Library, for the time and effort he devoted to locating material pertaining to the actions of H. L. Mencken, the precocious, twenty-three-year-old city editor of the *Baltimore Herald* during the fire. Thanks also to Joseph Eagan, manager of the Government Reference Service at the Pratt's Periodicals Department, who furnished scans of key pages from the 1904 editions of the *Baltimore News*.

I am also indebted to Nancy Perlman, who then was director of the research center and archivist at the Baltimore Museum of Industry. Ms. Perlman's team of research assistants unearthed many previously obscure items that turned out to be essential components of the story. At first, her research center seemed an unlikely repository of information, but under her direction it became an excellent source of material. Appreciation is also given to Theodore M. Chandlee, Jr., both a sponsor and able volunteer at the Baltimore Museum of Industry, who provided a personal insight on how his family's wholesale china and glassware business survived on the edge of the fire zone.

The New York Public Library's employees deserve recognition. Although understaffed, these New Yorkers came through with material on the role of New York City's fire department in fighting the Baltimore Fire. I warmly extend my appreciation to Glenn Corbett, technical editor, *Fire Engineering*, in Waldwick, New Jersey, for providing information about the Baltimore fire that appeared in 1904 journals having a nationwide readership. Articles he furnished from the weekly *Fireman's Herald* and *Fire and Water Engineering* proved valuable in developing details concerning the actions of out-of-town fire departments. Additional thanks go to Robin Waldman at the Jewish Museum of Maryland for sharing her expertise on the needle trades in Baltimore at the turn of the last century. In addition, many thanks to Tom Hollowak, librarian, Archives/Special Collections Department at the Langsdale Library, University of Baltimore, for information and leads on the life and career of Baltimore's youngest mayor, Robert M. McLane, perhaps the fire's most tragic figure.

My major source of material was the Maryland Historical Society, where Francis P. O'Neill, senior reference librarian, dispensed answers to almost any long-forgotten aspect of Maryland life. Robert M. Bartram, reference and access services librarian, helped greatly in hunting for old books and documents, while Mary Markey and Mary Herbert expertly located previously unpublished, century-old photographs that were both relevant to the story and of a surprising quality. Curator Jeannine A. Disviscour, and Assistant Curator Barbara Weeks, while engaged in preparation of the exhibition, "Baltimore Ablaze," proved helpful to me and gave freely of their valuable time as I worked toward completion of the manuscript.

Robert J. Brugger, history editor at the Johns Hopkins University Press, offered key insights on how to write a historical account. In addition, I owe much thanks to Neil A. Grauer and Stanley J. Modjesky for their advice and encouragement. In the early stages of the research, Charbel Barakat, a work/study student at Hopkins, found relevant material in the *Baltimore Sun*; many thanks for this effort. In the search for witnesses to the fire, I was fortunate to interview the late Thomas B. Turner, MD, dean emeritus of the Johns Hopkins University School of Medicine. Known affectionately as "Tommy," Dr. Turner—who passed away in 2002—recalled for me how his elders in Prince Frederick, Maryland, held him up when he was a toddler so he could see the fiery glow in the sky from the direction of Baltimore.

I also appreciate the assistance from Robert W. Schoeberlein, director of special collections at the Maryland State Archives in Annapolis, who gave freely of his valuable time to hunt with me for worthwhile illustrations from the Archives' vast collection of photographs.

Several years ago, when my colleague Susan Sadowski learned about my interest in the Great Baltimore Fire, she suggested I meet with Stephen G. Heaver, president and curator of the Fire Museum of Maryland. Steve has been most helpful these past three years, as has his staff. They went out of their way to dig up information and share leads about this landmark event in the history of Maryland firefighting. Particularly helpful were Debbie Brown, site manager of the museum, Jody Kloch, program coordinator, and Melissa Heaver, archivist. Numerous volunteers at the museum, experts in their own right, helped me during the research phase and later with verification of facts and figures. Noteworthy was Vernon B. Morris, Jr., along with Baltimore historian Wayne Schaumburg, who contributed to these efforts. Indeed, Wayne Schaumburg's excellent annual anniversary tours of the fire zone contributed to my interest and understanding.

At the Mercantile–Safe Deposit and Trust Company, Suzanne G. Wolff, director of community relations, and Trudy Frection, assistant vice president, trust marketing coordinator, helped me gain an understanding of how their venerable Maryland financial institution survived the fire and subsequently prospered. Recognition and thanks to Joanne Archer, then graduate assistant in rare books at the Maryland Room, Hornbake Library, University of Maryland, who located substantial information about the role and actions of the Maryland National Guard during the Great Fire and its aftermath.

At the Johns Hopkins University, Mame Warren supplied immense knowledge and insight into historical Baltimore photographs, producing many leads for finding rare, unpublished pictures. The Milton S. Eisenhower Library on the Homewood campus proved to be rich in information about Baltimore. While producing and distributing knowledge for the world, Hopkins is not lacking in historical information about its city. Thanks also to Joan Grattan of the Eisenhower Library's Special Collections Department and Archives for her assistance and insight into the collection of the papers of Hopkins' first two presidents, Daniel Coit Gilman and Ira Remsen. Both commented in their correspondence about the fire and its aftermath. James E. Gillispie, head of the Eisenhower Library's Government Publications/Maps/Law Library, and his assistant, Bonni L. Wittstadt, proved very helpful in finding old maps of Baltimore currently unavailable in electronic form. Within the School of Professional Studies, Charlene Walizer and Michael Houck supplied me with a constant stream of relevant and often difficult to find books from Hopkins' resources and interlibrary facilities. Thanks also to Andy Blumberg for his insights about the operation of Baltimore's trolley cars during the Great Fire.

In Baltimore's time of need, out-of-town fire departments rushed to its aid, and out-of-town newspapers furnished countless details and slants to the story not previously covered elsewhere. Modern technology provided access to these news stories but often left details that needed clarification. Archivists from the cities that aided Baltimore furnished important information and indeed often offered challenging leads that drew me to other departments and to exceptionally knowledgeable amateurs in their cities who covered their history as a hobby rather than an assigned function. Perhaps the most memorable of these tips occurred in Philadelphia, where Harry McGee, archivist for the fire department, clarified and verified information about Philadelphia firefighters and then suggested I contact "Scratch" in the police department. As I called the Philadelphia Police Department and asked for "Scratch," I felt like a character in a Peter Sellers movie. To my surprise, they not only knew Scratch, but after giving me his phone number announced that he had just walked into the office. The mysterious Scratch gave his e-mail address with the user name, "facesfromscratch." After corresponding via e-mail with him about various details for several days, I learned that he was a graphic artist who formulated faces of alleged perpetrators of crimes. Many thanks to Roderick Scratchard, who has a strong interest in the history of Philadelphia's police department and contributed details about the 150-member police unit that came to Baltimore during the fire.

As the time arrived to begin making sense of the story emerging from the vast amount of collected material, Frank Cappiello gave me that necessary push as I plunged into the writing. His continued support is greatly appreciated.

Thanks also to William Goodwin, chief of the Baltimore City Fire Department, Tom Asman, archivist of the Harrisburg Police Department, and Kenneth A. Bryson, Office of Public Information, Metropolitan Police Department, Washington, D.C., for their helpful information, advice, and intriguing leads.

Focusing during the past four years on research and writing sometimes diverted my attention from the day-to-day activities of being a professor. I appreciate the understanding and support from my colleagues. Particular thanks go to Dean Ralph Fessler of the Johns Hopkins University School of Professional Studies in Business and Education; Associate Dean Lynda de la Viña, director of the Graduate Division of Business and Management; Associate Dean Sheldon Greenberg, director of the Division of Public Safety Leadership; Professor Linda Randall, chair, and director, Department of Management; and Joseph McGowan, director of Federal Programs, Division of Public Safety Leadership.

In writing this book, the guidance of an

experienced editor of historical manuscripts was invaluable. Robert I. Cottom, publisher of the Press at the Maryland Historical Society, helped keep me focused on the text's overall objectives and skillfully edited this manuscript to bring out the best in the narrative without cutting necessary details. Working closely with Ric, David Prencipe, associate director for Imaging, Rights, and Reproductions, skillfully collected, processed, and in several cases identified images that added substantially to my efforts. Thanks also to Patricia Anderson, the press's managing editor, for cheerfully addressing day-to-day occurrences and to Joyce Wouters, marketing representative, for her keen insights. Many thanks also to James F. Brisson for his creative book design.

Very special thanks are due to Margaret Criscione, who has been my assistant for more than a decade. She is always one step ahead of me, anticipating the next challenges in the flow of work. I was most fortunate that she worked with me from the very onset of the research on the Great Baltimore Fire. Margaret is a meticulous person with a keen mind and a special knack for finding obscure papers, facts, and practically every note that I have written on the fire. She became so familiar with the subject and the evolving story that she needed little guidance and direction. Always willing to go the extra mile, Margaret Criscione is the most productive and efficient person I know. Indeed, more than any other person, she helped me with this overall effort. I will always be indebted to her.

Finally, my thanks, love, and appreciation to Jan, my dear wife of forty-eight years, who tolerated my absence and the disruption to our family as I tangled with the seemingly endless process of producing this book. Her encouragement and understanding continue to be an inspiration to me.

Pete Petersen
Johns Hopkins University
Baltimore, Maryland
October 2003

Chronology

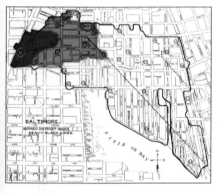

Sunday, 2:00 P.M.

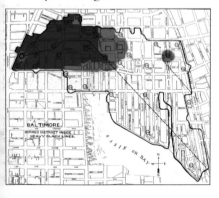

Sunday, 5:30 P.M.

Sunday, midnight

Sunday, 10:48 A.M. Fire alarm sounds at the Hurst Building, located between Liberty Street and Hopkins Place on the south side of German Street

10:53 A.M. Smoke explosion at the Hurst Building propelled fire south and west; however, wind from southwest spreads fire mostly to northeast

By noon, fires blazed in most of the area bordered by Liberty Street, Baltimore Street, Hopkins Place, and Lombard Street

Just after noon, Mullins Hotel, located on northeast corner of Baltimore and Liberty Streets, burns to ground in half an hour

By mid-afternoon, Fire breached Hanover Street and spread farther east

By 5 P.M. Fires burning in most of the area bordered by Liberty, Fayette, Charles, & German Streets. The exception being the northwest corner of this rectangle.

5 P.M. John Duer & Son building, located on Charles Street south of German is already ablaze when dynamited

6:40 P.M. Buildings dynamited on south side of West Fayette Street between Charles and McClellan

7 P.M. Dynamite planted in J. W. Putts's store at the southwest corner of Fayette and Charles Streets

Shortly after 7 P.M. Explosion in Putts's store spreads fire to Hall & Heading and Union Trust. Hall & Heading located on northwest corner of Fayette and Charles Streets, Union Trust located on northeast corner of Fayette and Charles Streets

7:30 P.M. Wind shifts now blowing from the west

7:30 P.M. O'Neill turns away dynamite team — building located at southwest corner of Lexington Street & Charles Street does not burn

7:30 P.M. Eastern edge of fire extends toward St. Paul Street

9 P.M. Bank of Baltimore, located at northeast corner of St. Paul and Baltimore Streets on fire

9:15 P.M. Herald Building, located at northwest corner of St. Paul and Fayette Streets on fire

9:15 P.M. Fire across street from Court House on northwest corner of St. Paul and Fayette Streets

10 P.M. Baltimore & Ohio Building on northwest corner of Calvert and Baltimore Streets ablaze

10:15 P.M. Sixteen-story Continental Trust Building, tallest building in Baltimore, on fire at southeast corner of Calvert and Baltimore Streets

At about 10:30 P.M. Fire burned at an extreme temperature (firefighters estimated 2,500 degrees) near Calvert and Baltimore Streets

Around 11 P.M. Wind shifted and started blowing from the northwest, reaching a speed of 30 mph. Consequently, the fire roared east down Baltimore and German Streets and southeast moving through the financial district and farther south toward the harbor

11:45 P.M. *Baltimore American* Building in flames at southwest corner of Baltimore and South Streets

Around midnight, Sparks jumped five blocks east and set Maryland Institute afire at Centre Market space at Baltimore Street

Around midnight, *Sun* Iron Building in flames at the southeast corner of Baltimore and South Streets

Monday, shortly after midnight, Church of the Messiah on fire at southwest corner of Fayette and Gay Streets

After midnight. Fire continued to move east on the south side of Baltimore Street to the Jones Falls. Then a 30-mph wind pushed the existing fires in a southerly direction toward the piers off Pratt Street

At 2:30 A.M. Fire expands in the southwest corner of the conflagration and also attempts to cross Charles Street below Lombard

3 A.M. Fire crosses Lombard Street and moves south to Pratt Street, also crosses Charles Street and advances to the east

4 A.M. Fire continues east along north side of Pratt moving almost to Jones Falls

During the early morning hours, one segment of fire makes a 180-degree turn at the Falls and moves west along the south side of Pratt Street almost to Bowley's Wharf

4:30 A.M. Powerhouse Annex, United Railway & Electric Company between Centre and Frederick Streets on the south side of Pratt destroyed by fire

5 A.M. Fire spread south on the east side of Charles Street to Balderston (small street parallel to and between Lombard & Pratt)

By 11 A.M. Almost every building along the west side of the Jones Falls from Baltimore Street to the northern edge of the Union dock was on fire or destroyed

Between 11 A.M. and 1 P.M. Firebrands & sparks ignited several fires on the east side of the falls; fortunately, firefighters extinguished the flames

1–1:30 P.M. & 2–2:30 P.M. Francis Denmead's malt house caught fire twice but firefighters extinguished the blaze on both occasions. Located east of Jones Falls at southern end of President Street

Three times during afternoon, lumber stacked on the Savannah Pier caught fire (Merchants & Miners' Transportation Company) located adjacent to Block Street and West Falls Avenue (situated west of Jones Falls)

Mid-afternoon, American Ice Company on West Falls Avenue became the last building ignited

5 P.M. Fire under control

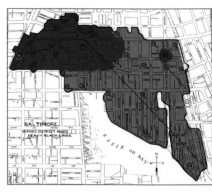

Monday, 3:30 P.M.

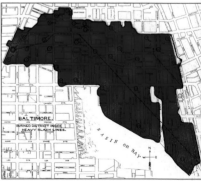

Monday, 5 P.M.

 X V

The Ever Present Danger

THE SMALL BLAZE THAT BEGAN on a frigid February morning in 1904 and swiftly grew into a conflagration may have been Baltimore's defining disaster. The Great Fire that consumed the center of Baltimore framed the future, not just for city businesses and municipal firefighting but also for the city's government and its citizens. Even a century later, the story of the fire that destroyed the heart of Baltimore and the city's remarkable recovery makes for one of the truly dramatic chapters in American history, and though the smoke cleared long ago, questions about the Great Fire still smolder. Exactly how did it start? Why did it spread so rapidly? Did Baltimore's fire department conduct itself heroically—or did it blunder? Did inept, ill-equipped firefighters, official incompetence, or tragic fate contribute to the extensive devastation? Why, at the dawn of the city's subsequent rebirth, did Baltimore's young mayor take his own life? What had gone wrong— and what went right?

Fire long had bedeviled Baltimore. In colonial times, fires constantly threatened the emerging town, whose wooden buildings were particularly vulnerable when heated with open flames during cold weather. Once a fire started, it could spread rapidly. Uncontrolled, raging fires frequently threatened major portions of the town and could cause substantial loss of life, inflict extensive property damage, and leave families destitute. Recognizing this danger, officials soon established regulations intended to prevent fires and improve fire fighting. In 1747, less than

FACING PAGE:
Fire in the warehouse of Henry Webb and Co. Oil on canvas, ca. 1830s MdHS

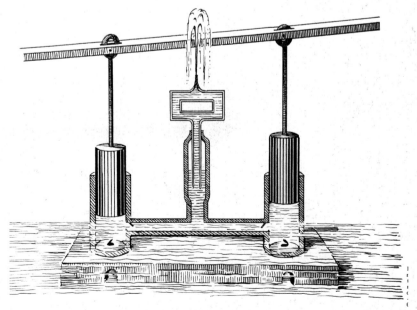

Diagram showing the operation of a basic hydraulic pump that employed a technology known "since the days of the Ptolemies in Egypt." Pushing the left plunger down squeezes water out of the left cylinder as the cylinder on the right fills with water. From Donald J. Cannon, *Heritage of Flames: The Illustrated History of Early American Firefighting* (Garden City, N.Y.: Doubleday and Co., 1977)

twenty years after Baltimore's founding, town commissioners required housekeepers to keep a ladder long enough to reach their rooftops, and ordered them to prevent chimney tops from emitting sparks. Residents soon acquired adequate ladders and began avoiding the use of highly combustible fuel—dried evergreen branches for example—in household fires, lest surging flames emit sparks from their chimneys. A ten-shilling fine chastened those who did not comply.

All citizens pitched in to fight fires. Homeowners tossed leather buckets into the road for citizen-firefighters to grab as they dashed to douse the flames in an endangered building. If a fire started at night, a quickly assembled band of vol-unteers, often led by two men, one with a torch and another with a horn, alerted neighbors to the fire and recruited additional volunteers to combat it.

In 1763 a group of Baltimore men organized themselves as volunteer firefighters. Six years later they spent ninety-nine pounds on a large, hand-powered pump to use as a fire engine. They purchased the device, which had been made in Holland, from a Dutch ship captain who initially did not want to sell it. Employing hydraulic principles used "since the days of the Ptolemies in Egypt," this simple device consisted of a leather suction pump inserted in a rectangular water tank. A solid cylinder or plunger pushed down on a slightly larger cylinder, squeezing water out a small hole. By having two water cylinders and plungers next to one another, the pump pro-

Dutch Fire Engine (1673). In 1769 Baltimore's volunteer firefighters bought a similar fire engine from a Dutch ship captain. From G. A. Daly and J. J. Robreecht, *An Illustrated Handbook of Fire Apparatus* (Philadelphia: INA Corp. Archives Dept., 1972).

Horse-drawn, steam-powered fire engine built in Baltimore in 1860 and used by volunteer firefighters. From *Three and Three Score Years, 1865–1928*, MdHS

vided a continuous operation: while one cylinder filled with water, the other discharged it. Enhanced by the addition of an attached hose—first introduced by Jan and Nicholas van der Heiden of Holland in the seventeenth century—the pump could spray fire-quenching streams over a substantial area, permitting firefighters to fight fires from a distance.[1] In addition to keeping it aboard to fight fires, the Dutch captain had used the pump to spray the ship's sails. Water caused the weave to shrink, which closed tiny holes in the fabric and made the sail more effective. Because the pump was quite heavy and cumbersome when filled with water, the Baltimoreans mounted it on a carriage for mobility. Dubbed "the Dutchman," this state-of-the-art device gave Baltimore a fire engine years before Boston, and even before Paris.[2]

In June 1799, city fathers expanded fire regulations by prohibiting the construction of wooden buildings within certain parts of the city, including the area bordered by Eutaw and Lexington Streets, the Jones Falls, and the harbor basin—by coincidence much of the area that would later succumb to the Great Baltimore Fire. The ordinance prohibited the construction of new wooden buildings in the central city by fining future builders of wooden buildings one hundred dollars for erecting the structure and an additional twenty dollars a month until its removal. Further, laborers who worked on the building had to pay one dollar for each day the builder employed them to construct it.[3]

In the nineteenth century, Baltimore's volunteer firefighters, like those in other rapidly growing cities throughout the United States, expanded greatly in numbers. For the most part, these men endangered their lives while providing a vital service to the community. Baltimoreans of the 1820s held volunteer firemen in high esteem and cheered enthusiastically as they passed in parades and demonstrated their strength, speed, and endurance during athletic events. With a strong sense of *esprit de corps*, each company was quick to defend its honor. Station houses became social

Baltimore City in 1862. This lithograph clearly shows the impact of the city ordinance of June 1799, which prohibited the construction of wooden buildings in the city. Brick and stone buildings are prominent. E. Sachse & Co. MdHS

In this 1848 lithograph, actor F. S. Chanfrau portrays "Mose," a mythical firefighter of Herculean proportions and the central figure in an 1848 play, *A Glance at New York.* "I'm bound not to run wid der machine anymore," Mose proclaims, though he was always drawn back to firefighting. The original caption adds, "Mose loved to fight, but did real volunteer firemen find pleasure in it too?" In fact, neighborhood bullies, brawlers, and drunks who joined volunteer fire companies earned these units a terrible reputation in the mid-nineteenth century. Photo #60446-B. Harry T. Peters, "America on Stone." Lithography Collection, National Museum of American History, Behring Center, Smithsonian Institution.

gathering places for many in the community, regardless of economic class. Insurance companies, community associations, and owners of buildings paid tribute to fire fighters for their death-defying heroism, honors that served to encourage the volunteers' continued service—and perhaps ensured the donors swift attention in the event of a blaze.

In time, the volunteers' eagerness to fight for their station houses or even the supposed honor of their fire engines began to wear on the public. The rising opposition to their boisterousness reflected Baltimore's growing refinement in the nineteenth century. In some cases, working-class rowdies had taken control of station houses and defied their leaders, undermining the teamwork needed to fight a fire. Some volunteer companies eroded their reputations further by fighting each other as much if not more than fires, competing to win praise and favors from wealthy property owners, and insurance money. Rioting among volunteer firemen in Baltimore became particularly violent, and for a time in 1847 firemen battled weekly. An especially vicious barroom brawl involving four firemen in 1849 ended in the fatal stabbing of one.[4] Citizens

might have tolerated drunkenness, womanizing, and loud profanity in the past, but by the 1850s many came to regard firefighters as brawlers and irresponsible drunks.

As did other American cities in those years, Baltimore decided to replace volunteer firefighters with a paid municipal fire department. By 1858 city leaders had determined that fighting fires should involve networks of responsible salaried professionals, sound zoning regulations, and adequate fire insurance.[5] In support of these efforts, Baltimore on February 15, 1859, organized six engine companies and placed them on active service. A seventh company came into being on March

Map of the Clay Street Fire of July 25, 1873, Baltimore's greatest fire until 1904. From J. A. Cassedy, *The Firemen's Record . . .* (1891). MdHS

KEY: A—Represents Thomas' Sash Factory.— Origin of Fire.
B. M. Banks' Silk Factory.
C and D—Dr. McCron's Church and parsonage.
E—J. D. Stewart's Livery Stable.
F—Dr. Smith's Second Presbyterian Church.
The darkened portion represents the Burnt District. The parts uncolored on Lexington and Liberty Streets, are houses where the fronts were saved and backs burned.

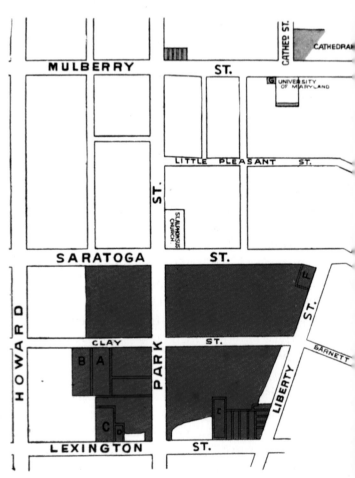

30 of that year. In creating the new department, Mayor Thomas Swann appointed a fire chief (called the chief engineer) to a five-year term. The chief had two assistant engineers and one fire inspector. Each of the engine companies had a foreman, an engineer, one fireman, and nine callmen. As might be expected, officials selected some of the best men from the volunteer companies to make up the nucleus of the newly formed, paid fire department. Regulations called for each company to have one steam fire engine, one hose carriage, a thousand feet of hose, twenty-seven horses, and a wagon outfitted with hooks, ladders, tools, and buckets.[6] In practice, the fire companies had to make do with much less equipment and far fewer horses. Shortages remained the rule throughout the early evolution of the Baltimore fire department.

In 1873 a large fire on Clay Street on the northern edge of the central business district just south of St. Alphonsus Catholic Church tested Baltimore's professional firefighters as never before. It erupted around 10:15 A.M. on July 25 in a box for wooden shavings in the sash and window blind factory of J. Thomas & Sons near the corner of Clay and Park Streets. The fire spread quickly. Unable to use the building's burning stairway, many of the 120 men and boys who worked in the factory injured themselves by leaping from second and third story windows in their frantic efforts to escape. Cinders from the intensifying fire spread the blaze by alighting on nearby dry shingle roofs. Far beyond the fire zone, the panic-stricken hastily and needlessly threw their furniture into the streets. Horse-drawn wagons helped evacuate household goods as well as ledgers and other important records and materials from endangered businesses. Before long, heavily laden wagons

jammed Charles Street, blocking other wagons that attempted to turn onto Charles from Saratoga Street. Farther west on Saratoga the heat was so intense that a wagon loaded with bedding burst into flames as it passed a burning building. Crowds formed quickly, and police divided their time between crowd control and catching looters. When the latter

"The Clay Street Fire—The Burning of the Central Presbyterian Church." From *Three and Three Score Years*. MdHS

"General View of Clay Street fire, reproduced from Frank Leslie's Weekly." From *Three and Three Score Years*. MdHS

became too numerous for officers to handle, police concentrated on recovering the would-be booty. Although most people leaving the area carried something, one evacuee seemed particularly quaint: a woman with gray curls made her way through the crowd with a china vase in one hand and a bird cage in the other.

Realizing his men would soon be overwhelmed, Baltimore Fire Chief Henry Spilman at 11:50 A.M. requested assistance from the nation's capital. Franklin Engine Company Number 2 and Columbian Engine Company Number 3 immediately loaded two steam fire engines, horses, hose carriages, and

eighteen hundred feet of hose onto three Baltimore & Ohio gondola cars, as firefighters clambered aboard a passenger car.[7] The train sped out of Washington and covered the forty miles to Baltimore's Camden Station in thirty-nine minutes, arriving only an hour after receiving Spilman's call for help. The District companies spent the rest of the afternoon fighting the fire, which was finally brought under control around 4 P.M. The Washingtonians stayed to put out scattered small fires and finally departed for home at 8 P.M. Ultimately, the Clay Street fire damaged or destroyed more than a hundred buildings. The burned area comprised the greater part

The Clay Street Fire
(1873). The view is looking
north from the corner of
Lexington and Park
Streets. St. Alphonsus
Catholic Church is in the
distance at left. MdHS

of four blocks bounded by Howard,
Lexington, Liberty, and Saratoga Streets.

The Clay Street fire was the largest crisis
Baltimore had faced since the Civil War. It
also demonstrated Baltimore's need for outside help when such calamities struck and
illustrated the challenges involved in placing
out-of-town firefighters alongside Baltimore's

The Clay Street Fire. View is from Park Street. From J. A. Cassedy, *The Firemen's Record . . .* (1891). MdHS

Clay Street Fire. The view is from Clay Street, though the direction is not specified, the day after the fire. Firemen are extinguishing a rekindled fire. From J. A. Cassedy, *The Firemen's Record . . .* (1891). MdHS

firemen. Strategically, the combined force managed to bring the fire under control by fighting it head on and confining it within a four-block area. Firefighters positioned themselves downwind and attempted to extinguish the fire as the flames bore down on them, concentrating on places they could save and avoided wasting resources and energy on buildings that were already hopeless. On this day, the tactic worked and limited the fire's reach.

City officials also learned the importance of a quick response that hot Friday morning in July 1873. In addition to moving his own firefighters well, Chief Spilman was quick to recognize the need for assistance. Indeed, he telegraphed for help only an hour and thirty-five minutes into this eight-hour fire. The fire also exposed the weaknesses of Baltimore's police force, which permitted wagons to race in and out of the fire zone, while in adjacent areas traffic jams impeded those trying to flee the flames. Additional police might have better controlled the crowd and prevented looting. Clay Street, the city's worst fire up to that time, gave Baltimore's fire department, police force, and city administrators valuable experience.[8]

Unfortunately, few Clay Street Fire veterans were still around thirty-one years later, when on a sleepy Sunday morning in February 1904, fire erupted in a warehouse near the central business district. Whipped by chilly winds, the flames grew into an inferno that raged out of control for the next thirty hours. City fires were deadly. About three hundred had perished in the Chicago Fire of October 8–10, 1871, and more than six hundred had lost their lives in that same city's Iroquois Theater Fire of December 30, 1903. Baltimore was about to meet the greatest threat from its most dangerous enemy.

The Great Baltimore Fire took on the dimensions of legend almost immediately. Not long after the blaze, H. D. Northrop wrote an account of both the Baltimore disaster and the Iroquois Theater Fire. Entitled *World's Greatest Calamities: The Baltimore Fire and Chicago*

"The Rescue." This wood–
cut from *Harper's
Magazine,* October 1877,
shows the esteem in which
firemen were held.
Courtesy, Enoch Pratt Free
Library, Baltimore.

Fire on Howard Street
north of Saratoga in 1890.
Urban fires like this one
tended to draw substantial
crowds. Note that the
stream from the firemen's
hose has reached the fifth
floor. That was rarely the
case during the great fire
of 1904. Firemen carry a
second hose up the ladder
to the rooftop. MdHS

On September 12, 1899, Baltimore's Engine Company No. 15 poses with its Holloway Combination Hose Wagon and Clapp & Jones Steam Engine on the St. Paul Street bridge. From *One Hundred Years of Baltimore's Fire Engines* (Baltimore: E. John Schmitz & Sons, 1971.)

Theatre Horror, Northrop's 1904 book offered thrilling accounts of both events but was short on accuracy. H. L. Mencken, in 1904 a young city editor of the Baltimore *Herald*, described his harrowing experiences during and after the fire in *Newspaper Days: 1899–1906* published in 1941. In a chapter entitled "Fire Alarm," Mencken entertained with an exaggerated account of various events connected with the fire, and noted that he always wanted to compile a substantial work about it "but the project got itself postponed so often that I finally abandoned it." Throughout the twentieth century, the *Baltimore Sun* and other papers published intriguing and accurate personal accounts and overviews, the frequency of which substantially increased in major anniversary years.

On the fire's fiftieth anniversary, Harold

Williams, a *Sun* feature editor, wrote *Baltimore Afire*, the first full account. In 1979, on the fire's seventy-fifth anniversary, Williams revised the book to describe modern-day Baltimore, including the soon-to-be-completed Inner Harbor. He also improved the accuracy of his statistics on the fire with new data that had come to light in that time. In 1992, Dean K. Yates described the role of the military in *Forged by Fire: Maryland's National Guard at the Great Baltimore Fire of 1904.* Yates filled a gap in the fire's history by providing previously unreported details of specific actions taken by the military during the blaze.

With the passage of time, more information has become available. Advances in information systems have facilitated retrieval of critical after-action reports, testimony, budgets, and commentary, circa 1904. When more than

"Start Your Water." Fireman calling to those tending the engine. From Charles T. Hill, *Fighting a Fire* (New York: The Century Co., 1897).

four hundred contemporary news articles, previously unassembled, were brought together they formed a story that could be followed and analyzed. This collection of articles also furnished both favorable and unfavorable opinions on Baltimore's handling of its great fire from a broad array of out-of-town journalists who reported from Baltimore, and from other eyewitnesses who hastened home after the blaze and told their local papers about what they saw.

One hundred years after the disaster swept through Baltimore, the use of the latest retrieval systems to unearth documents and first-person accounts offers surprising details about how this initially inconsequential fire nearly consumed an entire city. Venerable research facilities such as the Maryland Historical Society and the Enoch Pratt Free Library in Baltimore can now enable today's researchers to probe far more deeply into archival material that previously was murky at best, and to better answer key questions concerning the competence and actions of government leaders in response to the fire. The view from the fire lines is now clearer, too.

Baltimore Engine Company No. 15 and their Hale Water Tower photographed in 1900. MdHS

This photograph of buildings at Liberty and German Streets was taken in 1880. The wooden building at right was Friedrich Beier's Saloon, directly across Liberty Street from where the more substantial Hurst Building was later erected. Known in 1904 as Thomas Burk's saloon, it survived the Great Fire. Enoch Pratt Free Library.

Those who fought the conflagration, including units from the fire departments of twenty-four cities and towns, and approximately two thousand members of the Maryland National Guard, indeed faced myriad challenges.

In spite of the catastrophe, Baltimoreans and their businesses improvised, survived, and in many cases, thrived within just weeks of the fire, raising another question: How did Baltimore accomplish this stunning regeneration? In describing the fire and its aftermath, this book will address those questions.

"Hard Pulling." Baltimore firefighters responding to an alarm during the Great Blizzard of February 13, 1899. From *Three and Three Score Years.* MdHS

13

BALTIMORE.
BURNED DISTRICT INSIDE
HEAVY BLACK LINES.

BASIN OR BAY

1
Big Fire Here

ART SUMMERFIELD made his way along the quiet streets in the wholesale dry goods district of downtown Baltimore on the morning of Sunday, February 7, 1904. A wholesale clothing merchant with his headquarters in Durham, North Carolina, Summerfield had an opportunity that morning to conclude his business in Baltimore and get ready to move on to his clients in New York City. A southwest wind stirred the bitter cold as he neared the six-story brick building that housed the wholesale dry goods and notions firm of John E. Hurst and Company, located on the south side of German (now Redwood) Street between Liberty Street and Hopkins Place. The iron-fronted Hurst building, like others nearby, had dry goods piled inside, waiting for the spring visit of southern buyers. Summerfield looked up and spotted smoke pouring from windows on the fourth floor of the Hurst headquarters. "I was standing directly opposite the building when the fire was discovered," he recalled.[1] Summerfield assumed that only the fourth floor of the building contained the fire.

At the same time, Archibald McAllister, a private watchman and fire guard employed by several wholesalers to protect their warehous-

es, passed the corner of Hopkins Place and German Street. He saw smoke coming from a cellar grate in front of the Hurst building. Although the building stood empty of people that Sunday, a crowd began to gather outside. Moments later, firemen and their engines clattered into the street. "It seemed no more than two or three minutes before firemen and their equipment arrived," Summerfield later told a reporter.[2] When two firemen broke down a door on German Street, a thick cloud of black smoke burst forth, almost blinding them, followed by a loud roar as flames suddenly rushed upward. The draft caused by the open door was pushing the fire into every part of the building.

Unknown to Summerfield and McAllister, the fire they saw begin that frigid, windy morning would rage for nearly two days and become the largest municipal disaster in American history up to that time—requiring thirty hours to bring under control. And it probably all started with a discarded but still smoldering cigar or cigarette butt falling through a two-inch hole in a glass deadlight in the sidewalk above the basement of the

The John E. Hurst Company before the fire. MdHS

FACING PAGE:
Progress of the Fire. The numbers in circles show the hour of the fire, and arrows depict the direction and speed of the wind. *From 21st Annual Report of the Board of Fire Commissioners* (Baltimore, 1905).

15

Looking east on German Street as fire destroys the Hurst building. A crowd, many drawn by the smoke explosion minutes earlier, watches as firefighters attempt to contain the blaze. Their hoses can reach only the third story. MdHS

Hurst building. (During daylight hours, dead-lights provided some light to below-ground portions of structures, such as the Hurst company's basement.) At 10:23 A.M., fire department headquarters received an electronically transmitted trouble alarm from the basement of the Hurst building. Although trouble alarms were sent automatically and warranted continued attention, they often were caused simply by changes in water pressure and did

not usually require the dispatch of firefighters.

Twenty-five minutes later, however, at 10:48 A.M., when a heat-activated thermostat alarm in the Hurst basement rang, the firemen responded quickly. The 5th District Engineer, Lewin H. Burkhardt, led the initial response with the No. 15 Engine Company, No. 2 Truck Company, and the Salvage Corps. Captain John Kahl, commander of the No. 15 Engine Company, ran down Liberty Street

toward the building. Although he saw smoke coming from the windows on the Hurst building's top floor, he noticed that the alarm box located on the building's side indicated a fire in the basement. The firemen entering the building initially saw very little smoke on the first floor or in the basement—even though the fire appeared to be among packing cases on the lower level. They could see flames traveling across the basement ceiling toward the elevator shaft. This elevator shaft and a staircase in the center of the building provided a vertical fire draft from street level to the top of the building.[3] They attempted to fight the basement fire with a two-and-a-half inch water hose and a three-quarter inch chemical line. The system for the chemical line dropped a small quantity of sulfuric acid into a tank of sodium bicarbonate. The chemical reaction produced carbon dioxide, which placed the solution under pressure, allowing firemen to direct it onto the fire. But within minutes, dense smoke pouring down the elevator shaft blocked all visibility.

As Captain Kahl directed his firemen, he heard numerous doors slam throughout the upper floors of the building and thought a watchman was closing them. Actually, they slammed shut at the invisible hand of a strong draft— air expanding as a result of the fire's extreme heat. On hearing an ominous rumbling, the firemen began backing out the front door.

Sensing real trouble, Salvage Corps Captain Malcolm W. Jordan activated the nearest alarm box, number 447, at 10:51. Within minutes, District Engineer Burkhardt,

Sketch from the Utica *Saturday Globe* showing the collapse of the Hurst building. In actuality, three horses, led by Goliath, nearest the explosion, pulled a Hale Water Tower, not a fire engine, out of danger.

Between 4 and 5 P.M. Sunday afternoon the fire turned south from the Hurst Building and moved slowly down Hopkins Place against the wind. In the first photograph, smoke billows on the block of Hopkins Place north of Lombard Street. In the second, flames erupt from the upper stories of buildings a few doors from Lombard, while in the foreground, merchants empty their inventories into dray wagons. MdHS

the senior fire officer present, ran one block west to the corner of Howard and German Streets to sound the "four two's"—a third alarm from box 414.[4] Smoke continued to billow from the building, then suddenly a tremendous explosion shook the structure. "A sharp splitting roar went up with reverberating thunder followed by a peculiar whistling noise like that made by a shrill wind," a newspaper reported the next day.[5] This smoke explosion, also known as a back draft, occurred when oxygen re-entered the smoke-filled portion of the burning Hurst building. Only about five minutes had elapsed since the activation of the thermostat alarm.

The explosion abruptly and brutally informed the whole city that something terrible was afoot. Narrow streets, just thirty to forty feet wide from curb to curb, created a funnel for spreading flames as a brisk wind of approximately twelve miles per hour swept in from the southwest. Although Captain Kahl and the other firemen had escaped unharmed from the Hurst building, the explosion col-

lapsed some of its walls and crushed their Clapp & Jones Steam Engine No. 15, which they had been trying to hook up to a hydrant on the southwest corner of German Street and Hopkins Place.[6] Falling rubble also buried the steam engine's hose wagon, and demolished the No. 2 Hayes aerial ladder parked on German Street in front of the building. The horses attached to both the engine and the aerial ladder truck had just minutes before been unhitched and sent back to the station for more equipment.[7]

At about the same time, the calamity's first acknowledged hero appeared in the form of a fire horse named Goliath. As his team galloped north on Liberty Street, pulling a Hale Water Tower and a crew of firemen, the smoke explosion ripped the building. Goliath veered away from the reaching flames and in doing so drove his team and the fire crew out of the path of a falling Hurst wall, saving two other horses, the firemen, and the Hale Water Tower while being burned himself. Goliath would later become one of the best known

horses in Baltimore.[8] After the explosion, the Hurst building burned fiercely and the fire spread diagonally across to the northwest corner of German and Liberty Streets, where it ignited the Carr, Owens, and Heineman wholesale drug company.

Earlier, having retreated from the expanding fire, clothing salesman Summerfield was standing in Little Sharp Street about a block and a half from the Hurst building when he felt the concussion from the huge explosion in the store. "Over a dozen people around me were thrown flat on the ground by the shock. Others rushed in different directions and a stampede ensued," Summerfield told a *New York Times* reporter a day later, after he had arrived in New York.[9]

The narrow streets and increasingly intense flames and heat prevented firemen from maneuvering their equipment close to the burning buildings. Night watchman John A. Conlon in the National Exchange Bank located just across German Street, north of

the Hurst building, was keeping an eye on unfolding events from one of the bank's barred windows until the explosion blew it in. Knocked down, his clothing afire, Conlon jumped up and ran out of the bank, away from the fire and onto Baltimore Street, where he collapsed. A short time later he regained consciousness in Maryland General Hospital while lying next to another patient, S. F. Ball from West Fayette Street. Flying debris catapulted by the explosion had struck Ball as he was taking a Sunday morning stroll along Baltimore Street, a block away from the Hurst building.

Some onlookers speculated that gasoline had caused the mighty explosion, but actually the ignition of combustible gases precipitated the blast. This explosion greatly aided the fire's ability to spread by shattering windows in adjacent buildings and shooting firebrands into them, as well as onto nearby rooftops. As one of the first witnesses to the catastrophe about to begin, Art Summerfield firmly

In the third photograph, the flames have all but reached Lombard Street, and in the fourth, they have enveloped the Cohen-Adler Shoe Company on the northwest corner of West Lombard and Hopkins Place. The wind and the efforts of firefighters would prevent the fire from advancing across Lombard Street in this area. MdHS

The Manufacturer's National Bank on the northeast corner of Baltimore and Liberty Streets gutted by fire. MdHS

believed that "the fire could have been kept under control had it not been for the explosion in the store of Hurst & Co."[10]

Damaged by the explosion in the Hurst building and subjected to additional firebrands from the burning wholesale drug company to its west, across Liberty Street, the National Exchange Bank began to burn in full fury. The fire moved north along Liberty Street, consuming other buildings. When the fire arrived at 5 South Liberty Street, it lapped up Whitaker's Saloon, taking with it not only the sole source of income for the family that

owned the tavern but their home above it, too. Although the fire for the most part destroyed places of business rather than residences, the Whitakers were among the first of these unfortunate exceptions.

The fire leaped across streets and attacked neighboring blocks. A storage magazine filled with sixty pounds of gunpowder, kept—in accordance with fire regulations—on the sidewalk in front of Findlay, Roberts & Company, a hardware store, ignited next. The ensuing explosion across the street and east of the Hurst building tore off the fronts of several nearby structures and sent flaming debris into their now-exposed interiors. Spectators watching the initial expansion of the fire and its ensuing explosions said the firemen responded quickly and did the best they could but were simply overwhelmed by the blaze's rapidly burgeoning size and intensity.

An unlucky convergence of conditions then combined to feed what was quickly becoming a conflagration. In addition to the narrow streets and strong southwest wind, the haphazard construction of buildings aided the spreading fire. Many lacked safety glass. The result was that concussion from an explosion in one structure blew out the windows of nearby buildings, enabling firebrands to fly in and start new fires. Once the fire got inside a building, the ventilation and elevator shafts became ready conduits for it. Fires inside various buildings seemed to rise upward, while those ignited by debris that landed on the roofs of other structures quickly spread downward. The proximity of buildings spread new fires, and the narrow streets hindered firefighters' furious attempts to get in position in front of the blaze. Firemen appeared to have no problem getting all the water they needed, but their aging steam-powered fire engines could not propel streams of water much higher than the second story. Flames that reached beyond that range soared on without the possibility of water quenching their energy.

George W. Horton, Chief Engineer of the Baltimore Fire Department, dashed out of his house at 404 Colvin Street and arrived on the scene around 11 A.M. Positioning himself on German Street just west of Liberty, he sur-

veyed the rapidly expanding fire and tried to think of a way to stem it. As additional fire companies arrived, he sent them ahead of the blaze but quickly realized that his firemen needed help if they were going to save the city. Horton told Police Lieutenant Charles M. Cole to send a telegram to the

In this retouched photograph from the *Baltimore Sun*, a steamer pumps water on German Street near where the fire started. MdHS

In this photograph, probably taken early Sunday afternoon, police have established a cordon on Baltimore Street. Spectators in their Sunday finery straight from interrupted church services calmly watch the fire in its early stages. MdHS

BELOW
Merchants removing goods from their stores on Charles Street south of Baltimore Street on Sunday afternoon. Heavy smoke is but a block away. MdHS

Washington, D.C., Fire Department. Received in Washington at 11:40 A.M. it stated, "Big fire here. Must have help at once."[11]

Horton, in his late fifties, was a seasoned, stocky, tough-looking fire chief with a walrus mustache who had the respect and confidence of his men. He directed Pinkney W. Wilkinson, secretary to the fire commissioners, to summon all units. Wilkinson ran to Liberty and Fayette Streets and used a telephone in the Salvage

Police Marshal Thomas F. Farnan. MdHS

Chief Engineer George W. Horton was struck by a falling electrical wire an hour after the explosion in the Hurst building and did not rejoin firefighters until Monday afternoon. MdHS

Robert M. McLane, Baltimore's young mayor, initially refused to ask for help from other cities, and approved the proposal to dynamite buildings in the path of the fire in an attempt to create firebreaks. The decision proved disastrous. MdHS

August Emrich took over after Chief Horton was evacuated. Although he had two decades as a Baltimore firefighter, he lacked Horton's expertise as a chief. From *The Firemen's Herald*.

Corps Station to call the chief operator at fire department headquarters and tell him to sound a general alarm. When electronically transmitted by the Fire Alarm Telegraph Department, the general alarm to deploy all units puzzled some manning the stations that Sunday morning, who thought it might be a faulty signal. That wrong impression quickly faded as word of the fire spread rapidly throughout the city. Horton met with commanders of arriving units and city officials racing to the scene.

Art Summerfield, who had now moved farther north up Little Sharp Street, watched transfixed as the fire consumed the Hurst building within ten minutes of the back draft explosion. He also noticed that once-small

fires that had begun earlier in adjacent buildings had accelerated in another ten minutes, destroying two other clothing stores, Lowman & Co. and Daniel Miller & Sons. The wildest excitement, he remarked later, arose when people who had cash, important papers, and business records in their endangered offices tried to break through police lines to save their valuables. All feared that insurance companies would suffer excessive losses and be unable to pay fire insurance claims. Summerfield overheard business owners bitterly lamenting the loss of their livelihood and employees expressing fears for their jobs.

Not everyone who worked near the

Hurst building had the morning off that Sunday. Those who celebrated the Sabbath on Saturday normally worked from 8 A.M. until 2 P.M. on Sunday. Consequently, Sol Ginsberg & Company, a men's clothing manufacturer at 29 South Hopkins Place, had employees at work when the fire erupted directly across the street at the Hurst building. They wasted no time but began hauling away ledgers and other important business papers. In his hurried attempt to help to save the company's business records, Esther Wilner's father burst into their home at Sharp and Camden Streets four blocks south of the factory and dumped a load of heavy ledgers on the floor. The Wilners' house became one of several places where employees secured the Ginsberg firm's records. Esther recalled seventy-five years later that she had never seen her father look so intense and burdened. Out of breath, he grabbed her brother and started back to Ginsberg's factory to save more records, and, if they had time, bolts of cloth. "Don't let the children get into these records!" he shouted as he ran out the door.[12] The Wilners, father and son, retrieved several loads of cloth bolts before the police cordoned off the area and prevented them from returning to the factory. In time, it perished in the flames.

George Beadenkopf, an engineer employed by the Consolidated Gas Electric

Levin H. Burkhardt, Fifth District Engineer. MdHS

Light and Power Company of Baltimore, worked that morning as well. While riding on a streetcar nearing City Hall, he heard fire engines ringing their bells as they responded to the blaze. Looking out a trolley window, he could see a cloud of smoke to the west.[13] When Beadenkopf reached the corner of Charles and Fayette Streets, he heard the unmistakable roar of a fire out of control. After a quick inspection, he dashed to the Consolidated Company headquarters at 5–7 West Baltimore Street and climbed to the roof to observe the fire. There Beadenkopf found a large flaming piece of debris. He tossed it off the roof, but he and his fellow workers realized that fire soon would destroy their building and scrambled to gather and evacuate valuable company records. The company's general manager, Alten S. Miller, arrived as men from Spring Gardens, a Consolidated Company facility, using horses and wagons were hauling records to what appeared to be a safe haven in an old Consolidated Company building at 19 South Street, about three and a half blocks away.

As Baltimoreans learned about the fire, crowds began to form near the smoldering ruins of the Hurst building, in the vicinity of today's Baltimore Arena. Churchgoers hurried from their places of worship in mid-service to join the streams of citizens rushing downtown. Many still wore their Sunday best—frock coats and felt derbies—which they risked having set on fire by falling sparks and embers. For years thereafter, the expression "your hat is cooking" alluded to the havoc caused by the flaming debris raining down on pedestrians in the midst of the blaze.[14]

The dramatic sights and thrilling sounds of horse-drawn fire wagons rushing into action was a natural attraction, drawing people to the blaze and adding to their excitement once they arrived. That, too, aided the flames. On other days, police set up fire lines to isolate a burning area and prevent spectators from getting in the way of firefighters. On this Sunday, though, too many spectators rushed into the fire area too quickly, before police had a chance to establish their positions. Firemen soon found it difficult to accomplish even the most basic tasks, such as moving baskets of coal from fuel wagons to their steam-powered fire engines.

The mood of the crowd was perhaps predictably festive at first, but gradually it grew somber and restrained as the fire spread, threatening more and more of the city. The wind, still predominately from the southwest, continued to carry firebrands and sparks to adjacent blocks, setting fire to awnings, roofs, and any exposed flammable material. The fire was quickly surpassing any attempt at control. Chief Horton had no sooner directed firemen to focus their efforts on a fire at the Roxbury Rye Company at 115 West Baltimore Street than the building collapsed. Horton's firemen had not even begun to deploy.

Just before noon, George M. Upshur, president of the Board of Police Commissioners, was summoned to his office in the mammoth, four-year-old city courthouse, located on the block bounded by Calvert, Fayette, Lexington and St. Paul Streets. Because the two other members of this board, John T. Morris and Edward H. Fowler, remained at home due to illness, Upshur assumed full authority to act as a board-of-one. He first directed Police Marshal Thomas F. Farnan to order the immediate closing of all places selling liquor in the city. Upshur also considered requesting units of the Maryland National Guard to assist the Baltimore police. Before deciding on that, however, Upshur sought additional assistance from the police departments in Washington, Philadelphia, York, Pennsylvania, and New York City.

Around noon, the city's young mayor, Robert M. McLane, and key members of his staff arrived on the fire scene. McLane's party consisted of Benjamin T. Fandall, city engineer; Edward D. Preston, the city's chief building inspector; and Joseph L. Wickes, street cleaning commissioner. McLane led his entourage through the fire area. Firemen were dashing one way and merchants and factory owners the other as the thirty-six-year-old McLane viewed the extent of the damage, then hurried to the Salvage Corps Station and conducted an impromptu meeting. They struggled with the mayor's grim query: How can we stop the fire? Preston made the unprecedented recommendation that a demolition crew use dynamite to clear paths that would act as firebreaks to contain the blaze.

As the fire began moving north around noon, Chief Horton was standing at Liberty and Baltimore Streets, a block north of the now-vanished Hurst building, when a live trolley wire fell and burned him. Horton was painfully but not seriously injured. Dr. Edwin Greer, the fire department surgeon, gave the chief opiates to relieve the pain and insisted on his leaving the scene. He was carried in a patrol wagon to No. 23 Engine House on Saratoga Street near Howard Street, where he remained in a semi-conscious condition until Monday morning. Horton relinquished his command to District Engineer August Emrich, an up-and-coming member of the fire department. Emrich assumed command until about 1:30 P.M. Monday when Horton returned, except for a short time when he also had to leave his post because of a smoke injury to his eyes. District Engineer Burkhardt filled in for Emrich for this short span.

When McLane first learned of Horton's injury and evacuation, he sent a carriage to the home of former chief William C. McAfee with a message asking him to take charge of the fire. McAfee at first refused politely, but then, remembering an old political grudge, added, "City Hall can burn down too!"[15] Within an hour, though, McAfee's sense of duty overcame his personal objections and he returned to the fire department, though not as the chief. He began offering tactical advice and went out to the lines himself to direct the placement of hose streams and encourage his former subordinates. Later in the day, in what one newspaper called "a desperate effort to save a lot of warehouses on the waterfront," McAfee led a detachment of men "on a burning wharf to throw dangerous resin barrels in the river." Actually McAfee went to the waterfront to supervise the loading of vats of turpentine on barges. They would be towed down the Patapsco River and dumped overboard.[16]

As word spread and the gravity of the emergency became apparent, business owners and managers dashed downtown to their offices and attempted to save as much as they could from the approaching flames. After seizing cash and negotiable instruments, they tried to save accounts receivable ledgers, accounting records, and customer lists. In some cases they only had time to grab a handful of valuables. As the fire moved relentlessly in the direction of the city's banking center, depositors small and large hurried to rescue their cash and the contents of their safe deposit boxes. Panic-stricken depositors who pounded vainly on the locked doors of banks soon discovered what the bankers already knew: time locks prevented entry to the banks until Monday morning.

Learning about the fire just before noon,

Henry F. Rinn rushed downtown to rescue what he could from his small office and music shop located near what had been the Hurst building. Quickly arriving on the scene, he found that the building had already started to burn. Policemen prevented him from running inside to save what he could.

Yet what might have been total disaster turned into an opportunity for Rinn, who in addition to operating a fledgling music store had begun augmenting his income by dabbling in the emerging picture postcard business. Already popular in Europe, picture postcards had just started to catch on in the United States. Fortunately, Rinn had his five-by-seven-inch view camera, tripod, and a supply of sensitized glass plates with him, rather than in his now-burning office. Rinn made pictures by developing and drying glass plates in his bedroom, placing them over sensitized contact paper, then throwing up the shade for a few seconds, exposing his images to the light. However primitive his methods, he managed to produce some good photographs of the city in his tray of developing fluid.

The fire-fighting commotion made it difficult for Rinn to set up his tripod on the congested, smoke-filled streets, let alone concentrate on taking pictures. Horse-drawn wagons carrying desperate owners of burning buildings could easily trample pedestrians who already had to watch out for slush, ice, falling wires, and tangled hoses underfoot. Ideal sites to take gripping photographs were hazardous, while safer places offered few possibilities. Rooftops offered great panoramic views but usually offered little drama to record. Rinn nevertheless managed to dart along the narrow streets between blazing buildings, evade the fast-moving wagons, and somehow avoid police attention. Perhaps his camera and tripod gave him some sort of legitimacy, serving as a pass for roaming the fire zone at will. Street-smart and quick on his feet, Rinn captured dramatic photographs that today remain the most compelling record we have of the Great Fire. After recording vivid scenes of the blaze and its aftermath on his glass plates, Rinn sent finished photographs to a firm in Milwaukee and in about ten days received stacks of picture postcards to sell in Baltimore.[17]

Additional quick-thinking entrepreneurs soon recognized other ways to turn calamity into cash. With a strong demand for transport to carry material being evacuated from the fire zone, aggressive quick-buck artists responded promptly. They found horses and wagons, sometimes their own, and appeared on the scene as desperate business owners searched for a way to move their valuables. Teamsters bargained with the frantic businessmen, who sometimes engaged in curbside bidding against one another for a wagon. Hoping for a rapid turnaround that would enable them to pick up other loads, teamsters moved businessmen's records, small safes, and other valuables out of the fire zone and dumped them quickly in a readily available place for safekeeping. The shadier among them demanded payment in advance, then disappeared when the businessmen dashed back into the building for another armload of valuables. Some business owners safeguarded the cargo in the wagon they had hired by standing in front of the horse until their own workers finished loading the goods.

Larger and more established organizations tended to fare much better when they evacuated their property. One such organization, the Consolidated Gas & Electric Company, routinely dealt with storms and disruptions at odd hours; in fact, many of its employees worked unconventional shifts. They also had little difficulty functioning during a crisis, and had plenty of transportation equipment readily available. Meter and appliance wagons pressed into service at the height of the fire moved valuable records from the company's downtown offices to power stations on the outskirts of Baltimore. Many of these records, such as detailed maps of the location of gas mains, would be critical during the reconstruction of the city. In order to help the firefighters, the B&O Railroad sent a gondola car loaded with fifty tons of coal to the vicinity of Pratt and Howard Streets. Volunteers—women as well as men—hauled the coal in wheelbarrows and baskets to the fire engines.[18] Volunteers also aided small businessmen and those who lacked resources. In many cases, people of good will helped strangers save what they could, securing these valuables in their houses and those of nearby friends.

People recalled looking down a block and seeing flames hop from rooftop to rooftop. Elegant cast-iron building fronts bent and collapsed in the intense heat, exposing the buildings' interiors to the hungry flames.[19] As the blaze moved farther to the north and east, the fire seemed to be concentrating in an area bounded by Liberty Street, Baltimore Street, Hopkins Place, and Lombard Street. Mayor McLane had hoped that the fire would not reach the north side of Baltimore Street, but just after noon, the Mullins Hotel at the northeast corner of Baltimore and Liberty Streets caught fire. Fortunately, the hotel's managers had demonstrated remarkable prescience at the very beginning of the fire at the Hurst building, anticipating the potential danger and evacuating the hotel guests at least two hours earlier.

The first contingent of firefighters from the District of Columbia arrived at

Baltimore's Camden Station at 1:30 P.M., less than two hours after Horton's plea for assistance. Crammed onto a hastily arranged, chartered B&O train, they had sped between Washington and Baltimore in a breathtaking thirty-eight minutes, almost beating the existing record of thirty-six minutes. B&O workers together with bystanders at Camden Yards helped the Washington firemen unload their horses and equipment. As the capital's Number 3 and Number 6 Engine Companies charged out of the station, crowds of Baltimoreans lining the streets cheered them. Effectively deploying the Washington firemen proved more challenging. Acting Fire Chief Emrich seemed almost overwhelmed by the task of leading all of Baltimore's firefighters, not to mention the new arrivals, as they struggled against the advancing fire.

Assigned initially to Little Sharp Street, the Washington firefighters seemed to have a clear mission in view, but without warning they found themselves checked before they could begin. American cities at the turn of the century had different fireplugs—more than six hundred different sizes and variations of fire hose couplings across the country. The problem was simple: Baltimore hydrants would not accommodate Washington hoses. The Washington firemen tried wrapping canvas bandages around the couplings in order to attach their hoses to Baltimore's fireplugs, but that did not work. They and fire companies from other cities discovered that they had to get dangerously close to the fire before they could bring their weak streams of water to bear on the flames.

Isaac George, a student at Georgetown University home for the weekend, watched workers at the Jackson Company's wholesale dry goods and notions store on the south side of Lombard near Liberty Street labor mightily to save their building. Blazing structures on the north side of Lombard gave off so much heat that the paint already had peeled off the Jackson Company's building. In an effort to cool their building so it would not catch fire, the Jackson Company workers draped wet blankets over the edge of the roof and kept them saturated with water drawn from the roof's tank, a typical feature atop buildings of the period. The tactic worked. By keeping the blankets soaked, they saved their building from igniting. Returning to Georgetown by train that night, Isaac George could look to the north and see a red glow in the sky all the way from Baltimore.[20]

Baltimore's citizenry pitched in to help the embattled firemen move their heavy hoses from one fire-fighting position to another. Firefighters usually had to abandon any hose covered by falling walls, debris, and live electrical wires. The need for additional hose became clear by the early afternoon. George W. Gail, president of the Board of Fire Commissioners, ordered board secretary Pinkney Wilkinson to find more—fast. "Get more hose. Get all the hose you can." Wilkinson telephoned three companies in New York City and ordered a total of sixty thousand feet of hose with the first segment of 10,000 feet due in Baltimore the next day. With entire blocks of buildings now burning, the situation seemed hopeless for firemen who had just a few streams of water with which to battle the blaze. Aged members of the Veteran Volunteers, an organization of one-time firefighters from the days of Baltimore's volunteer stationhouses, grabbed two vintage hand engines from the group's headquarters at 9 Harrison Street and promptly put them back in service, "playing two good streams on the fire," according to one account.[21]

Chandlee, Quarles & Co. on the southeast corner of Hanover and Lombard Streets after the fire. Observers watched the fire from its roof. Other buildings around it burned to the ground. MdHS

Realizing the battle could well be lost, Acting Chief Emrich decided to change his tactics. He directed his forces to concentrate on extinguishing new fires as they started outside the inferno. To combat the embers and firebrands thrown from the massive blaze, sweepers and bearers of water buckets manned rooftops on the outskirts of the fire, particularly those of public buildings such as the courthouse, post office, and City Hall. Baltimore physicians accustomed to rushing to an emergency rallied to the cause by reinforcing fire department surgeons and treating injured firefighters for cuts, bruises, smoke inhalation, and electric shocks from dislodged trolley and live electric wires. When Baltimore police captain Bernard Ward suffered a neck burn because the heat of the fire had ignited his celluloid collar, all of his men quickly removed their own collars.

The fire continued its inexorable march north and east. Hanover Street appeared for a time to be the eastern boundary. By mid-afternoon, though, the fire had breached Hanover Street and spread farther east. McLane and his secretary, Harry W. Rodgers, watched its progress as they stood at Hanover and Lombard Streets. When the fire leaped across Hanover, they knew that the situation had entered an even graver phase. H. P. Chandlee Sons, Company, a wholesale china and glassware firm on the southeast corner of Lombard and Hanover Streets, barely escaped the flames as large buildings burned fiercely right across the street. A prominent supplier of fine dinnerware to hotels and restaurants throughout the southeastern United States, Chandlee took special pride in providing the distinctive blue table services for the Royal Blue, a B&O deluxe train that traveled between Washington and New York City. When the Chandlees first learned about the fire, they had jumped into a horse-drawn wagon at their West Baltimore home on Elgin Avenue in Walbrook and hurried downtown. As a precaution, they took the company records home for safekeeping. Later, reporters and other observers took advantage of the view from Chandlee's roof, with many taking photographs of the fire from this seemingly safe vantage point. Fortunately, as the leading edge of the fire approached them, the winds shifted. With this loss of momentum, the fire did not travel

John W. Putts's department store at 10 North Charles Street, on the southwest corner of Charles and Fayette, was known as the "Glass Palace." He finally agreed to let his building be dynamited when it caught fire, but the explosion sent flaming debris into adjacent buildings. From *Men of Maryland* (Baltimore, 1905).

south of Lombard Street in the vicinity of Hanover.[22]

As the fire spread, the Consolidated Company's old building at 19 South Street no longer seemed a "safe haven." Before dark, volunteers moved piles of the firm's business records and maps to the company's Canton Station. They then considered the possibility that the fire might reach eastward all the way to the Jones Falls. If it did, the exposed gas mains crossing the Jones Falls would be in great peril. Immense amounts of gas would escape as the lead joints of the pipes melted in the heat, gas that not only would fuel the fire's momentum but also drain a key source of power and illumination throughout the city. In anticipation of this potential disaster, the gas company quickly moved to re-activate its gas producing operation in Canton, which had been closed since production had been moved to Spring Gardens.[23] This prompt action averted a major calamity and prevented other parts of the city from losing their gas supply.

Nothing could help the streetcars, though, when the supply of electric current to them failed at 4:00 P.M. The trolley crews stayed with their stalled cars, sustained by the food and coffee brought to them by their families, and by complete strangers who lived along the streetcar routes.[24]

Meeting with fire and police officials as well as business leaders, the mayor proposed taking a drastic step. Citing Preston's earlier suggestion that buildings be dynamited in order to form open areas that would act as barriers to the advancing fire, McLane said he intended to begin by blowing up the block formed by Hanover, German, Charles, and Lombard Streets. The debate over who would pay for this deliberate, calculated demolition immediately became as intense as the fire

Demolition crew poses after the fire with cases of dynamite lying in the street. MdHS

itself. Building owners, concerned that their fire insurance would not cover destruction by dynamite, argued that they should not have to suffer the loss. Others contended that if the city dynamited their buildings, responsibility should fall on the city, and the city or its insurance company should have to compensate them. Still others argued that they would be saving the city and insurance companies from further loss by consenting to the dynamiting of their buildings to halt the fire. Therefore, if blowing up their buildings helped stop the blaze, insurance companies should compensate them.

As the argument continued, a thousand pounds of dynamite, only slightly protected by a covering layer of dirt, arrived by horse and wagon from Anne Arundel County. For

Laying a fuse for dynamiting. *Philadelphia Inquirer*, February 10, 1904. MdHS

 3 1

more than an hour it sat on Lombard Street, east of the fire now advancing across Hanover Street. The crowds of spectators who had gathered to witness the fire's spectacle became more cautious when they heard about demolition crews planting explosives. John Duer & Son, located on Charles Street south of German, occupied one of the first buildings to be dynamited. The place was already ablaze when at approximately 5 P.M. the demolition crew set off the dynamite inside. Contrary to everyone's expectations, the building did not collapse. A heavier charge detonated in the Schwab Brothers building on the southwest corner of Charles and German Streets had

even more disappointing results. Instead of leveling the building, the explosives dug a deep hole in the ground and blew out the windows in buildings nearby. Soon the whole block was on fire. The demolition crew continued its efforts undaunted but had little success in leveling a dozen or more buildings on Lombard, Baltimore, and Charles Streets.

Around 6:40 P.M., another round of dynamiting began with two or three more buildings along West Fayette Street, but again blasts intended to block the fire seemed only to spread it. Arriving at the southwest corner of Charles and Fayette Streets, the demolition crew hoped to level J. W. Putts & Co., a four-story department and notions store with a substantial glass front and side windows. With approval from the owner, the dynamite crew ignited several charges on the West Fayette Street side of the building, just as it started to burn. The explosions blew out the windows of the Union Trust building diagonally across the intersection and sent firebrands and sparks barreling north across the street, igniting the Hall and Heading building and the attached Slessinger Shoe Store. A few moments later, the Union Trust building also stood ablaze.

Upon hearing of the demolition plans, Thomas O'Neill, owner of one of the city's largest department stores, became determined to save his business, located in the building north of the burning Slessinger Shoe Store and Hall and Heading department store. When the dynamite crew arrived, they found the stocky, red-headed, fifty-four-year-old

O'Neill blocking the doorway in his Sunday best. He was adamant. The dynamite crew would put no charges in his building. Pointing to his protective firewall and an exterior sprinkler system that sprayed water outside the building next to exposed windows, O'Neill persuaded the firefighters to spare his store. The odds were long, but his gamble paid off: O'Neill's survived the fire.

Police Commissioner Upshur, who had previously requested and received assistance from other police departments, next contacted Brigadier General Lawrason Riggs, commander of the Maryland National Guard's First Brigade. All of the National Guard and Naval Reserve forces fell under the direction of General Riggs. Placing the military in charge of overseeing the fire zone while the police protected the rest of the city simplified the tasks of both.

Photograph taken at 8:27 P.M., about the time the Bank of Baltimore, on the northeast corner of St. Paul and Baltimore Streets, burst into flames. MdHS

Long before fire threatened structures along the harbor basin, the fireboat *Cataract* joined the fight against the fire in downtown Baltimore. Moving into position near Pratt and Light Streets around 7 P.M., the *Cataract* attempted to shoot water into the fire. Firefighters laid about 2,000 feet of hose from the boat, reaching as far north as German Street, but wagons on Pratt Street soon cut the hose to ribbons. The *Cataract* fought on, undaunted.

Late Sunday evening, the commandant at Fort McHenry contacted Police Marshal Farnan to offer assistance. Farnan indicated that fire threatened several federal government buildings, including the federal courthouse across from the municipal courthouse on Calvert Street, the post office at Fayette and Calvert Streets, and the customs house under construction on Gay Street. He immediately sent thirty Regular Army soldiers on horse-back to the fire zone. With bayonets fixed, they set up a barrier across Fayette Street where it crosses Calvert Street and settled in to guard federal facilities.

The constant dash of horse-drawn fire wagons, and mounted police added to the sense of urgency, while in the background, the constant tolling of the bell at City Hall gener-ated a feeling of panic for some, but not all. Esther Hillman's family, living at Sharp and Camden Streets, prepared to move in case the wind shifted to the south. The children all slept downstairs as Esther's parents poured water on the roof to extinguish falling sparks. Seventy-five years later, Esther recalled: "I remember my father on the roof and my mother on the sidewalk down below, filling the bucket and tying a rope to it, so the men could pull it up."[25]

Workers evacuated patients from City Hospital (now Mercy Hospital) on Calvert Street in ambulances, a number of them military vehicles from the Fourth and Fifth Maryland National Guard Regiments. Some of those evacuated had already been uprooted earlier, having been sent to City Hospital from another hospital closer to the fire. Approximately three hundred patients moved from their beds to be distributed among Johns Hopkins, Maryland General, St. Joseph's, and University Hospitals.

Buildings burned fiercely along German and Lombard Streets. The intense heat ignited both the wooden paving blocks and asphalt on the thoroughfares, turning the streets into rivers of flame. To the north, buildings along Baltimore and Fayette also stood ablaze. According to one witness, "The roar of the flames sounded like the wind howling on a mountain top."[26] Having consumed the supposedly fireproof Union Trust building at

Charles and Fayette Streets, the fire moved directly east, destroying buildings along East Fayette as it advanced on the headquarters of the *Baltimore Herald* at the corner of St. Paul and East Fayette Streets. When the Herald building and those next to it on St. Paul Street caught fire, attention turned to the courthouse across the street. Workers there frantically moved records into vaults and transported furniture, drapes, and books to the Juvenile Court located in the middle of the courthouse. Fortunately, a shift in the wind around 11 P.M. saved the courthouse from destruction.

The manager of the Western Union

office felt secure in the "fireproof" Equitable Building at Calvert and Fayette Streets, even as the blaze approached from the west. He dashed from the building only at the last moment, when ordered out by the police. Much to his amazement, the Equitable Building quickly became an inferno.

Rosa Kohler and her family lived at 329 North Carrollton Avenue in a three-story rowhouse with a white stoop. Three-quarters of a century later, she recalled worrying that Sunday night about her father, who worked in the Western Union office in the Equitable Building. After the Equitable Building began to burn shortly after 9 P.M., displaced Western

Photograph taken from the Maryland Trust Building at 1:30 P.M. Sunday, showing the fire at Sharp, Hanover, German, and Baltimore Streets. From Daniel McIntyre Henderson, *The Book of the Fire*, 1904. Enoch Pratt Free Library.

Firefighters in the inferno on Baltimore Street about 1:30 P.M. Sunday. Note how the overhead wires diffuse the streams before they can reach the fourth floor. MdHS

Union workers set up a transmission office in the attic of the House of Welsh Restaurant on the northeast corner of Saratoga Street and Guilford Avenue, north of the fire zone. On Carrollton Avenue where the Kohlers lived, neighbors kept a vigil to spot large, flying embers that might start a fire on their roofs, and set up a bucket brigade to wet housetops all along their block. In the midst of all this activity, Rosa's mother seemed to disappear. Though out of danger from the fire and apparently safe for the moment, Rosa grew frantic.[27]

When the fire, moving east along Baltimore Street, reached St. Paul Street, the intense heat projected across the street to the Central Telephone Exchange at 7 St. Paul, where operators were working long hours that Sunday as part of an expanded shift of forty switchboard employees. Two sisters, Mary and Annie Winkler, were among those operating Baltimore's phones. In an effort to prevent panic among the operators and keep them at their posts to maintain critical service as long as possible, phone company supervisors closed the drapes on the office windows

37

Wreckage of a Cast-Iron Front Building. From *Scientific American,* February 20, 1904. MdHS

on the pretext that doing so would reduce the glare on the switchboard signal lights. This effectively blocked the operators' view of the approaching fire. As the heat from across the street intensified, the windows in the Central Exchange cracked. Sparks and embers landed on windowsills, and operators wrapped themselves in wet blankets as a defense against the heat. Despite the rising temperature and imminent danger, they continued to place calls for frantic customers. Finally, around 9:20 P.M., the building caught fire. With little time to spare, the operators' supervisor, Anne Schmidt, led the operators to safety through an existing passage into the Calvert Building and then to an exit leading to Fayette Street. Once outside, they hurried eastward, assembling at the corner of Fayette and Gay Streets.

Because supervisors had not told the evacuating operators the scope of the danger, some had the impression they would return. Mary and Annie Winkler watched helplessly as flames engulfed the Telephone Exchange building, and suddenly realized they had left their purses behind.

Before long, wagons transported the Winkler sisters and the other operators to another telephone exchange north of the fire zone. For the next three weeks, the high volume of calls meant that operators worked especially long hours. Mary and Annie Winkler often found themselves working round-the-clock shifts. A man from the telephone company came by their house at North Avenue and Gay Street to pick up a suitcase containing clothing and personal effects for each of them, so that when they finally went off duty, they could stay near their posts and sleep on cots furnished by the National Guard.[28]

As the fire moved east, the Baltimore & Ohio Railroad Building at the northwest corner of Baltimore and Calvert Streets caught fire about 10 P.M. Fifteen minutes later, flames shot up the tallest building in Baltimore. Previously proclaimed fireproof, the sixteen-story Continental Trust Building became the hottest place in the two-day conflagration, with an estimated temperature of 2,500 degrees Fahrenheit. The Maryland Trust Building joined the blaze of skyscrapers on the northwest corner of Calvert and German Streets. From the Eastern shore, southern Maryland, and the northern counties of Virginia, people could see the glow of Baltimore's burning skyscrapers.

Looking at the fiery spectacle, E. Louis Shipley, District Engineer No. 6 said, "A thousand fire engines cannot stop it, the fire is king tonight."[29] The fire at the Carrollton Hotel seemed particularly intense. Located at the northeast corner of Light and German Streets, it added to the substantial blaze now under way in an area bordered by St. Paul and Light Streets on the west, Fayette Street on the north, Calvert Street on the east, and German Street on the south. Fortunately, many of the guests from the Carrollton Hotel departed about 2 P.M. for other hotels and places of lodging, or simply decided to leave Baltimore altogether.

Governor Edwin Warfield, a portly, distinguished-looking former newspaper publisher and businessman with a white mustache and goatee, arrived by train from Annapolis at 10:15 P.M., just as the Continental Trust Building was bursting into flames. He had arranged to accompany Annapolis firefighters on their run to the city earlier in the day, but when he failed to arrive at the Annapolis train station on time they had left without him. A *Sun* reporter had interviewed him on the train and later wrote that the worried Warfield had been trying unsuccessfully since 5 P.M. to call and telegraph his office in the Fidelity Deposit & Trust building. Although he served as the state's chief magistrate, Warfield continued in his capacity as president of the Fidelity Deposit & Trust Company, which he had founded in 1890. "Not only my own securities but those of others are kept there," Warfield said as the train raced towards Baltimore.[30]

The wind, which had been blowing from the west since about 7:30 that evening, shifted around to the northwest about 11 P.M. The fire briefly seemed to stall, no longer moving north, though the blaze continued to be intense along Baltimore and German Streets. Then wind began to guide the fire toward the south, in the direction of the financial district and the harbor basin. As the first day ended, sparks reached the historic Maryland Institute in Marsh Market Space on Baltimore Street—five blocks *east* of the main conflagration—and set it afire.

Governor Edwin Warfield arrived from Annapolis Sunday night greatly concerned with the fate of the Fidelity Deposit & Trust Company, which he had founded in 1890. MdHS

39

Looking west on German Street as firefighters attempt to halt the forward edge of the fire. The ruined building at left is the National Exchange Bank, damaged and set aflame by the smoke explosion in the Hurst building, out of the picture to firemen's left. Enoch Pratt Free Library.

40

The Great Baltimore Fire 1904

2

Must Have Help at Once

COMPANIES OF FIREFIGHTERS from near and far came to Baltimore to join the battle. Much initial public attention focused on the Washington units, who arrived less than two hours after the fire began only to learn that their hose couplings did not fit Baltimore's hydrants. But small firefighting units from such then-remote communities close to downtown Baltimore as Westport, Roland Park, Highlandtown, and Hamilton were also among the first to arrive. On hearing the smoke explosion in the Hurst building at 10:53 A.M., they reacted as they normally would and set out to lend a hand. Under long established protocol, it was relatively easy to get outside help—Baltimore's chief merely telegraphed his counterpart in another city for assistance. The chief providing the assistance, however, normally checked with his own mayor or, in the case of the District of Columbia, the commissioner. Municipal pride and politics were also a consideration. Since it was common for out-of-town firefighters to disparage the ability of the endangered city to fight its own fires, an embattled fire chief and mayor would often think twice before seeking help from another fire department.

Chief Horton had requested assistance from Washington on his own, but when his assistant, August Emrich, replaced him, Mayor McLane involved himself. McLane, who had been elected only eight months earlier and initially was reluctant to ask for help from other cities, actually declined offers of support until much later on Sunday, when the situation in Baltimore had become almost hopeless. Then he implored others to send help right away. Before the fire was over, portions of twenty-four fire departments from throughout the mid-Atlantic states joined the fight to extinguish Baltimore's fire. Maryland contingents came from tiny Sparrows Point (not then part of Baltimore), Annapolis, Relay, St. Denis, Havre de Grace, and Westminster. From Pennsylvania came mighty Philadelphia and its smaller neighbors, Chester, Hanover, Harrisburg, Altoona, Phoenixville, York, and Columbia. From New Jersey, came Trenton's firefighters and Atlantic City's heroic volunteers. Delaware sent Wilmington's firefighters, and from Virginia came Alexandria's men. All joined forces with sizable contingents from New York City and Washington.

Four major cities came to aid Baltimore. Washington provided five engine companies. Philadelphia, second to arrive, furnished eight

FACING PAGE:
The fire in a place not specified but probably quite early. MdHS

more. Wilmington arrived next with four engine companies. New York City's department was the last to arrive but came with the most men and equipment: nine engine companies and a hook and ladder company. All endured significant challenges as they attempted to help Baltimore—and each other.

WASHINGTON, D.C.
— *"Further Assistance Not Needed, Fire Under Control"*

Washington D.C. Fire Chief William T. Belt responded swiftly to Baltimore's call for help. Courtesy, *The Fireman's Herald*.

When Chief Horton's 11:40 A.M. telegram— "Must have help at once."—reached Washington, Fire Chief William T. Belt relayed, the message to Commissioner Henry B. F. Macfarland, president of the District of Columbia Board of Commissioners, who was attending Sunday services at Washington's Church of the Covenant, on Connecticut Avenue and N Street Northwest. Leaving the church without delay, Macfarland telephoned the fire department and instructed Belt to "do everything possible" to aid Baltimore.[1] Belt had moved quickly. On receiving Horton's telegram he had alerted four engine companies for a possible run to Baltimore. As soon as Belt received Macfarland's go-ahead, Engine Companies No. 3 and No. 6, numbering twenty men, loaded their equipment onto a train comprising an engine, a boxcar for the horses, and four flatcars. Pulling out of the District's rail yards at a few minutes past

noon, the train raced the forty miles to Baltimore on a clear track with the throttle wide open. It arrived at 12:37 P.M. Chief Belt, Fire Marshal Sidney Bieber, and the capital's coroner, a potentially grim participant, accompanied the firemen.

B&O Passenger Agent H. P. Baldwin traveled with the train to Baltimore and upon returning to Washington told a *Washington Post* reporter, "When we were at Relay, about nine miles from Baltimore, we saw the black smoke and flames leaping far above the city."[2] Baldwin said he believed that about ten thousand people cheered when they arrived at Camden Station, and he noted approvingly the advance preparations for unloading their apparatus. One Washington company rushed to the vicinity of German and Liberty Streets, where the fire had started. The men in the other company assembled about five minutes later and joined the first company as both moved farther north, fighting the fire near Little Sharp and Baltimore Streets. Baldwin proudly told the *Washington Post* that as Washington's firefighters "dashed down the street cheers challenged in volume the noise the fire was making."

Despite the crowd's applause, the frustrating fact that the District's hose couplings would not fit Baltimore's hydrants complicated the Washington firefighters' efforts. "Chief Belt was forced to run the hose down into the sewer," Baldwin lamented, as he pointed out the lack of a standard hose coupling and hydrant size. Washington's fire engines also had trouble finding sites where they could set up and fight the flames because the collapsing brick walls of gutted buildings formed barriers as they fell into the street. To make matters worse, an abundance of falling electric and trolley wires, some of them live and dangerous, hampered attempts to clear this rubble.

By early Sunday afternoon, the fire had reached north to Baltimore Street and began moving east with a shift in the wind. Burning debris has ignited the roof of the eight-story building of L. Greif and Bros., a men's clothing manufacturer, at center. Firefighters are unable to send water above the second floor. The building with the three circular windows on the top floor is Ades Bros., a manufacturer of umbrellas, at the corner of Hanover and West Baltimore Streets. MdHS

By three o'clock, the fire has moved farther east on Baltimore Street to Hanover Street. A steam engine hooks up to a hydrant as the fire moves toward the photographer on Baltimore Street. MdHS.

According to the next day's *Washington Post*, the failure of "the United Railway & Electric Company and United Electric Light and Power Company to turn off their current proved a serious obstacle."[3]

Early Sunday afternoon, as the Washington firefighters battled the blaze, Commissioner Macfarland sent a telegram to Mayor McLane: "National Capitol deeply sympathizes with Baltimore. Was glad to send fire department assistance. Call upon District government for anything else it can do." Later that afternoon, Macfarland received a response to this offer: "Further assistance not needed — fire under control."[4] By Sunday evening, however, Baltimore's situation was becoming desperate, with the glare of the fire now visible forty miles away in Washington. Swallowing his pride, McLane requested addi-

tional help from the District. A second B&O train, carrying Engine Companies No. 2 and No. 8, led by Foreman Carrington, left the capital at 10:30 P.M. and dashed to Baltimore to join Belt's contingent already deployed. "Other trains were crowded with hundreds of people who went to Baltimore for business interests or [to] view the spectacle," the *Washington Post* reported the next morning.[5] Late Sunday night, as Washingtonians learned that Baltimore's fire still raged out of control, throngs of people hungry for news gathered near the *Washington Post* bulletin boards. A rumor circulated that two firefighters from Washington's No. 6 Engine Company had been killed while fighting the fire and that one of the fire engines from the District had been crushed by falling walls. Commissioner Macfarland immediately demanded that

Looking east down
Baltimore Street at Liberty
Street, in the fire's wake,
late in the afternoon on
Sunday. MdHS

Baltimore conduct a detailed inquiry into
these reports, even as the fire raged on. He
received word from the burning city early
Monday morning that officials could not
confirm the rumors and believed that all the
firefighters from Washington were safe.[6]

Although Macfarland wanted to assist
Baltimore, he also had to look out for the
welfare of the men he had put in harm's way.
Satisfied with their condition, Macfarland
ordered a fifth engine company to join them
at 2:30 A.M. Monday. Since McLane was
spending most of his time out in the streets
rather than in his office, communicating with
him was difficult. Macfarland decided to go
to Baltimore to see for himself what was
going on and learn how the District could
render additional assistance. Taking cash from
his office's coffee fund in case he had to cover
unexpected expenses, he left Washington by
train at three on Monday afternoon and
arrived in Baltimore an hour later. For the
next two hours he tried to find McLane and

visit Washington's firefighters as they fought
the flames. Circling around the flames,
Macfarland went directly to City Hall, now
on the northern edge of the fire zone, only to
find that McLane was not in his office.
Macfarland then went to the southeast portion of the burning area, where his men were
battling the flames. He visited the different
companies, met with Fire Chief Belt and all
the foremen, and shouted words of encouragement to all of the firefighters with whom
he came in contact. They were exhausted,
smoke-begrimed, and hungry, but proud to
help their brothers in Baltimore. To counter
the effects of dropping temperatures and the
strong wind, Macfarland arranged for District
Fire Marshal Bieber to provide the men with
a constant supply of sandwiches and hot coffee, thereby putting the money from his coffee fund to good use. An engaging politician,
Macfarland lost no time in speaking with
groups of Baltimoreans clustered around the
fire's periphery and quickly passing along to

Firefighters direct protective streams of water at Vogeler, Son & Co. (left) and Thomas Burk's wooden saloon (right) on the west side of Liberty Street at German Street. The Hurst building (right), the Merchants' Protective Credit and Collection Bureau (with turret) and the National Exchange Bank (left distance) are in ruins. MdHS

his men the warm praise he had heard for the Washington Fire Department and Chief Belt. He also told Washington's firefighters that they were in the thoughts of their friends back home. Since Washington's companies deployed first in the critical area near where the fire started and later served as part of the last line of defense against the raging blaze, Macfarland firmly believed Baltimoreans appreciated their assistance.[7] As he returned to the capital, the Washington firemen were holding back the fire on the west side of the Jones Falls. Although the fire eventually did

cross over the falls in several places, it did not cross where the men from Washington held the line. On departing, Macfarland demanded to be notified if any of his men suffered injuries.

A. J. Lee, a clerk in the executive branch of the District government, also traveled to Baltimore to check on Washington's firefighters and talk with Chief Belt. "The District firemen extinguished the first blaze that started in the lumber yard district [Monday afternoon] and were successful in preventing a spread of the flames," Lee later told the

Washington Post. He also noticed that even though he "was suffering keenly from exhaustion and exposure," Belt was constantly in the center of the action, directing operations and cheering on his men. Belt had been soaked with water the day before, "his eyebrows were singed, and his eyes [were] full of cinders [that] caused him considerable pain," Lee told the paper.[8]

Fire Marshal Bieber, who had accompanied Washington's firefighters to Baltimore on Sunday, returned to the capital at two o'clock Monday afternoon and reported that "the men were all safe and their work was accomplished at the highest order," but "Chief Belt was tired out and wanted relief." Commissioner Macfarland directed James Kelliher, Washington's assistant fire chief, to go to Baltimore and assume control of the District companies. After they had brought the main fire under control at about 5 P.M. Monday, the Washington firefighters went about stamping out the secondary fires. By 11 P.M. Monday, a special train was getting ready to return Engine Companies Nos. 3 and 6 and a portion of No. 2 Company to the capital. These units had been in continuous service, and when the train arrived in the District, all of the men were sound asleep. The District firefighters remaining in Baltimore returned home on Tuesday, February 9.

PHILADELPHIA
— *"A Blizzard from Hell"*

When Philadelphia director of public safety David J. Smyth learned about Baltimore's conflagration around noon Sunday, he tried but failed to contact Baltimore's mayor and chief of police by telephone. He then contacted Philadelphia fire chief James C. Baxter and arranged with the

B&O to have transportation ready for Philadelphia's firemen. The railroad responded quickly with a special train, but the men took more than an hour to load it because of difficulty in hoisting engines onto open, flatbed cars. The firemen initially took their engines to 24th and Chestnut Streets, but because this loading area lacked inclined ramps, they hurried over to the sloped ramps at 24th and Race Streets. Whipping the huge horses to spur them on, they tried to haul the heavy loads up the steep incline, but the weight of the engines dragged the teams back each time. They next went to Arch Street, where the ramps were not so steep and the engines could finally be loaded. Smyth also assembled a group of 150 Philadelphia police officers, each equipped with boots and a rubber overcoat, in anticipation of a request from Baltimore for further assistance.

Around 2 P.M., about three hours after the fire started, Smyth sent a telegram "offering every aid that lay in Philadelphia's power" only to receive a reply from Baltimore that it needed no additional assistance. However at 6 P.M., he received a different—and cryptically desperate—telegram: "Send all help possible. Pennsylvania Railroad."[9] Philadelphia's leaders had anticipated as much. Even before they received the urgent request for help, four engine companies were on their way south, led by Assistant Fire Chief Edward A. Waters. Police Captain David McCoach and 150 policemen departed for Baltimore a little after 8 P.M. on a special Pennsylvania Railroad train out of the Broad Street Station. The Philadelphia contingent also included two physicians and several stable bosses.

The departure of a large group of policemen caused "all sorts of rumors to fill

Philadelphia Assistant Fire Chief Edward A. Waters. Courtesy, *The Firemen's Herald.*

Baltimore Hose
Company No. 15 at
Manufacturer's
National Bank, dousing
smoldering embers.
MdHS

The damage seen from Monument Square. The Battle Monument, commemorating Baltimore's role in the War of 1812, stands at left. The fire raged through the area shown about 10 P.M. Sunday. MdHS

the air as to the emergency" that called for their presence. A crowd collected around City Hall and the Broad Street Station, hoping to learn more. At the 13th Street Station, workers took a waiting flatcar carrying an engine and its hose cart and hitched it to the special train of police officers, which then sped off to Baltimore. Five officers arrived at the station "just in time to see the train's rear lanterns disappear through the train yard."[10] Receiving word just before 10 P.M. that the fire still was unchecked, Philadelphia dispatched two more engine companies to Baltimore. At about 11 P.M., another special train pulled out of 13th and Market Streets and raced south.

Waters and his four engine companies arrived in Baltimore around eight o'clock Sunday night, to be met by an appreciative crowd. Baltimore's firemen were exhausted after fighting an unrelenting fire since eleven that morning. Despair was setting in. Winds shifting from the west and later the north gave the fire new momentum, but the Philadelphians charging into action brought new energy and enthusiasm to those fighting it. Moving initially toward the northeastern portion of the fire zone, they fought the fire as it advanced east and then turned south through the business district. Reinforced around 3 A.M. by three additional engine companies and now seven companies strong, the Philadelphians tried to get around the fire to the south, hoping to block the approaching wall of flame, but the fire was too strong.

Foreman Thomas O'Brien of Philadelphia Engine Company No. 11 accompanied Companies 11, 43, and 21 as the fire

The B&O Railroad Building. From H. D. Northrop, *World's Greatest Calamities: The Baltimore Fire and Chicago Theatre Horror* (n.p.: D. Z. Howell, 1904).

backed them toward the harbor. Stationed initially about two blocks north of the wharf, the companies fought desperately as the flames pushed them ever farther south until they found themselves at the end of a pier and at the water's edge. "We thought our end had come," said O'Brien of that brutal night. "The flames were licking about us, the heat was intense and the smoke stifling. There seemed to be but one chance for life, and that was to jump overboard. Fortunately, the wind changed, and we were able to get off the pier."[11]

Courage and daring were evident in other actions by Philadelphia's firefighters that equally cold Monday. "There is no doubt," said Michael Welsh, foreman of Philadelphia's Engine Company No. 20, "that in saving the big plant of the National Biscuit Company, the Philadelphia firemen also saved at least a dozen other properties." Welsh had reason to boast. When Engine Company No. 20 started to protect the National Biscuit Company's plant "one of the Baltimore firemen offered to bet $5 that they could not remain on the street corner with their engines," related Welsh. The Pennsylvanians accepted the wager with gusto, Welsh laughed, and "the Baltimore man backed down and thereby saved $5."[12]

On returning to Philadelphia, tired men "told vivid tales of the terrible fire." "It was the greatest night I ever saw in my life," said fireman William Young. "A hurricane wind carried clouds of ashes and lurid sparks that resembled a blizzard from hell," said another. "It was a picture that I believe even Dante never dreamt of." L. H. Crosby, a New York salesman who watched Philadelphians in action, extolled their grit. "Philadelphia can be

Firemen spray water on the
smoldering B&O Railroad
Building after the fire.
MdHS

Men from Philadelphia Engine Company No. 11 returning home from Baltimore on February 9, unload their engines from railroad flatcars. Unlike their earlier dash to Baltimore, they had little difficulty finding an adequate loading ramp. From the *Philadelphia Inquirer,* February 10, 1904.

proud of her firemen," said Crosby. "Within ten minutes after the companies arrived, they were ready." Said another eyewitness, "They fought the flames from in front until their clothing caught fire."[13]

HARRISBURG
— "Send all the engines and companies that you can spare"

As the fire raged out of control late Sunday, Harrisburg's Mayor Vance C. McCormick received a request for assistance from McLane shortly after 10 P.M. "The outlook is so bad that I would ask that you send all the engines and companies that you can spare," McLane wrote. Responding as best they could, Harrisburg showed what a mid-sized city could do in the face of catastrophe. Mayor McCormick, Police Chief Col. Joseph B. Hutchison, and Fire Chief George W. Lutz quickly held an emergency meeting and decided that although they had five steam fire engines, they could safely send only one. In the event that a major fire somehow erupted in Harrisburg, a special train would remain in Baltimore to bring the loaned engine home.

Members of the city's Hope Fire Company gathered their apparatus and dashed to the rail depot at the foot of Third Street, where the train was being loaded. Workers secured the engine onto a flatcar while the horses traveled in the boxcar and a group of fifteen firefighters and two policemen rode in the coach. Crowds of curious spectators gathered at the station. Some who tried to accompany the firemen in the coach had to be "hustled out before the train prepared to leave." At 12:30 Monday morning, the train chugged out of Harrisburg and down the Northern Central line for Baltimore, a trip that ordinarily took about two hours. Putting on all its steam, the train "established a new high speed record of 97 minutes between this city and Baltimore," the *Harrisburg Telegraph* reported proudly.[14]

When the Harrisburg contingent arrived in Baltimore at 2:07 firefighters and railroad workers unloaded the engine and nine hundred feet of hose at a siding north of the Calvert Street Station, with the hose going right onto waiting wagons. Baltimoreans had become adept at helping with the unloading of out-of-town fire departments, and drew favorable comments from the Harrisburg men.[15] Baltimore officials met the incoming trains and directed the disembarking firefighters and their engines and apparatus to critical points on the fire line. When Harrisburg's Hope Company deployed, the main concern was stopping the fire from moving south to the docks or east where it could cross the Jones Falls and spread to Little Italy, the Jewish community, and even Fells Point.

The Hope Fire Company fought alongside companies from Washington, Philadelphia, Chester, and other cities, battling the advancing flames for hours. "There were seven [engines] at one corner pumping at capacity speed trying to force an opening into the advancing wall of fire," reported the *Harrisburg Patriot,* but the high wind drove the fire from building to building. For their protection, the men had to withdraw their engines to a position a block away from the blaze. The only times the Hope engine stopped working while in Baltimore were during two brief "intervals of time required in making the changes of [fire] plugs." Reports that the engine "had blown up, that it had to suck up salt water and that the Baltimore water supply had been exhausted were entirely groundless."[16] At 2:30 Monday afternoon, Sergeant Charles O'Donnell, in charge of his city's police detail in Baltimore, notified Colonel Hutchison in Harrisburg that the fire was under control, only to discover on returning to the fire scene that the fire had broken out again right in front of the Hope Fire Company. Once more, the Harrisburg men were fighting a fire that was out of control.

As word spread through Harrisburg of the magnitude of the Baltimore fire, crowds gathered anxiously around the *Patriot's* offices to read its bulletin board and learn the latest news. Phone lines were busy with calls to Baltimore as Harrisburg's citizens tried to keep abreast of events. Eagerness to report information led to a number of false stories in local newspapers. A rumor on Monday had it that "the Hope fire engine had blown up while in service in the streets of Baltimore," generating much fear. Fire Chief George W. Lutz, assured in a message from Sergeant Charles O'Donnell, that the fire "still [was] raging and engine still in service," attempted to squelch the erroneous report, only to prompt another one. Harrisburg's mayor, seeking to dispel the Hope Engine explosion rumor, explained, "The engines were sent to the water front, where they were obliged to pump salt water." Since firefighters did not pump the salt water through a filter, he went on, it foamed and "this no doubt created an impression that the engine was about to blow up."[17] In fact the engine did not pump salt water.

The *Harrisburg Telegraph* printed another false story about a fallen firefighter from York, Pennsylvania. "Jacob Ilgenfritz of the Laurel Fire Company of York, Pa., was killed about 5 o'clock this morning [Monday] at Baltimore and Frederick Streets." According to the unfounded rumor, Ilgenfritz was fighting a fire at the Schuler Clothing Company "when the wall of the building fell. Ilgenfritz was caught under the wall and was dead when found." The paper even reported that the dead man "was forty-five years old and said to be married."[18]

The anxiety of Harrisburg citizens fueled the rumors, as they desperately waited to hear more about these terrible events. By 10:30 Sunday night they could see an eerie glow in the southern sky. In an attempt to learn the extent of damage, many Harrisburg residents jumped on trains, including a number of entrepreneurs who had financial interests that were being threatened and possibly ruined in the Baltimore business district. Adding to the excitement in Harrisburg were eyewitness accounts from people returning home. John C. Kindler, assistant fire chief and in charge of Harrisburg's firefighting detail in Baltimore, related the story of the wild and thrilling ride the night before as the firefighters raced through southern Pennsylvania and into Maryland. While not a stop was made en route, "there was danger at times that the steamer would be hurled from the flat car as the special [train] dashed around the sharp curves at mile-a-minute speed," Kindler told the *Telegraph*. Although Common Councilman Augustus H. Kreidler, who had accompanied the men to Baltimore, did not know when they would return, Harrisburg Fire Chief Lutz "sent 12 members of the Hope Company to relieve [some of] those who went down."[19]

When Harrisburg's men returned from Baltimore shortly before midnight Monday night, they had puffy eyes after constant exposure to smoke and "showed the effects of long service without sleep and not being able to get any time to remove the black from their faces and hands." After cleaning up their engine, hoses, and other apparatus, cleaning and feeding their horses, and taking a most welcome bath and a hearty meal, they reminisced about the two times in Baltimore that large buildings fell near them. As a result of one building collapse, "John Ilengelfritz of Laurel Company of York was injured," but not killed, as had been reported. In addition, "George Shuler of our company was injured by a piece of falling timber and several of our members overcome by smoke."[20] Both men returned to work after brief medical treatment. Indeed, given its narrow escapes from collapsing buildings, the Hope Fire Company

felt fortunate in having sustained no serious injuries.

NEW YORK CITY
— *"Where Can We Fight for You the Hardest"*

According to a possibly apocryphal account, about 12:45 A.M., Monday, February 8, New York firefighters raced to the Liberty Street Ferry pier to extinguish a fire on the ferryboat *City of Baltimore*. After dealing with a surprised and puzzled ferryboat crew, and realizing there had been an error in communications, the firefighters regrouped and prepared for what would turn out to be a trip to the city of Baltimore.[21]

When word of the fire in Baltimore reached New York Sunday afternoon, George McClellan, mayor and son of the Civil War general, telegraphed McLane and offered to dispatch some of New York's firefighters to help. As of 1 A.M. Monday, he had received no response. Half an hour later, McClellan decided to approve Acting Fire Chief Charles W. Kruger's plan to have the Pennsylvania Railroad ready a train to Baltimore.[22] Across the Hudson River in the Jersey City rail yards, from which southbound rail service left the New York area since no bridges or tunnels yet existed to provide a land connection to Manhattan Island, railroad workers readied the train and stood by. With still no word from Baltimore, McClellan decided not to wait any longer. Leaving their station houses at about 1:45 Monday morning, seven engine companies raced to the piers and boarded ferries that set off for Jersey City about 3 A.M. The engine companies were No. 5, stationed at 340 East Fourteenth Street; No. 7, from Beekman Street; No. 13, at 99 Wooster Street; No. 16, stationed at 223 East Twenty-Fifth

Street; No. 27, from 173 Franklin Street; No. 31, located at White and Elm Streets; and No. 12, at 261 William Street. Many of the men had never been far from home; a few admitted that their travels from Manhattan had been limited to excursions to Coney Island in Brooklyn, and to Hoboken and Weehawken in New Jersey. Some who awoke in their firehouses did not know the purpose of the early morning call. They expected only an ordinary fire and left unprepared for a trip out of town, much less to faraway Baltimore. A spot check of one group revealed that not more than one in ten was wearing socks when they boarded the ferries that frigid morning.[23]

When the ferries tied up at the Jersey City terminal, horses pulled the engines to the rail yards where a train dispatcher named J. Vanderhoff had prepared nine flatcars to transport the apparatus. It took about three more hours to load and lash the engines. Horses and their drivers rode in two boxcars while the rest of the firefighters rode in two coaches at the rear of the train.[24] In the rush to assemble the contingent, the railroad separated the passenger coaches from the locomotive with flatcars, thus preventing the locomotive from heating the two coaches. Eight reporters boarding the train to accompany the New York firefighters noticed the unusual location of the passenger coaches at the rear of the train and reckoned that a locomotive racing behind the train could ram their coach. Each man quietly purchased an accident insurance policy from the agent at the station. Twenty-five cents for a twenty-four-hour policy that provided $5,000 worth of coverage suddenly looked like a wise investment for such a perilous journey. Unfortunately for the eighth reporter, the agent refused to sell more than seven policies for the same train—there were limits to the risk an insurance company was willing to take.

Leaving the Jersey City yards at 6:34 A.M., the New Yorkers received their first greeting when they passed trainloads of commuters near Newark. Rousing cheers from strangers would continue throughout the trip. As the train rumbled south and the unheated cars grew colder, the stentorian voice of one fireman filled the frosty air with the song "Mike Murphy the Fireman."

> She held in her arms a bundle in white,
> And sang to her baby in the fire's ugly
>   light.
> Mike Murphy was a fireman.
> With a prayer in his heart and an oath on
>   his tongue
> He managed to reach them, there where
>   they hung.
> Mike handed them down to the man on
>   the ladder,
> And he died in his duty, but the world ain't
>   no sadder.[25]

Despite the lack of heat, Battalion Chief John P. Howe, in charge of the expedition, looked out for his men's safety and comfort. In Philadelphia, where the B&O provided huge sandwiches and hot coffee, Howe served his men before having something himself. Dr. Harry M. Archer, a renowned local fire-fighting buff, bought food for the firefighters, paying almost one hundred dollars out of his own pocket to feed them. The New Yorkers invited Archer to accompany them.[26]

Back in New York, Mayor McClellan learned something of the extent of the devastation in Baltimore and decided to send two additional engine companies and a hook and ladder company. A second train carrying Engine Company No. 26, stationed at Thirty-Seventh Street between Seventh and Eighth Avenues; No. 33, from 42–44 Great Jones

Falling walls of the Hurst building crushed this parked Clapp & Jones steam engine belonging to Baltimore's No. 15 Engine Company. Just minutes before the incident, the horses had been unhitched and sent back to the station for more equipment. Spectators soon gravitated to the site to have their photographs taken with the wreckage.
MdHS

Street; and Hook and Ladder No. 5, stationed at 96 Charles Street, soon left the Jersey City rail yards.[27]

As the second New York train raced south, the first had to stop when two covered axle boxes on the overloaded train overheated from excessive friction. Proceeding after the boxes had cooled, the train had another mishap only six miles from Baltimore. The first flatcar, containing engines Nos. 7 and 13, jumped the track at a switch and derailed. Restored to the track, the train had gone about a half-mile when the firemen spotted smoke billowing into the sky. "It looks like new smoke," one veteran observed ominously. Arriving in Baltimore at 1:50 P.M. the tired and cold New Yorkers on detraining had their spirits lifted immediately by the sight of thou-

sands of cheering Baltimoreans there to greet them. Art Summerfield, who stood in the crowd and traveled later that day to New York, told a reporter, "I was much pleased when I saw the New York firemen get into town." Had they "not arrived the fire would have spread to the Post Office building," Summerfield said.[28] August Emrich also expressed relief on seeing the New Yorkers. Howe asked Emrich, "Where can we fight for you the hardest?" Emrich replied, "Our men are about played out and the fire is sweeping toward the warehouses and the docks. If these go, God help us." Howe said, "Send us there, and we'll do what we can for you." Emrich directed them to the southeast part of the fire zone and the most critical task in fighting this great fire—stopping the blaze from crossing the Jones Falls, expanding, and then moving farther east into the tenements of Little Italy and eventually Canton. Howe and his firefighters worked their way through the devastated parts of Baltimore to the warehouse district. "Those warehouses are doomed," Howe proclaimed, "but we'll save the docks and the shipping and lumber yards or bust."[29]

Indeed, much remained for the New Yorkers to accomplish as they arrived in the heart of the fight. To the east, on the far side of the Jones Falls, sparks and embers had caused a stack of lumber to burn in the vicinity of President Street and Canton Avenue. From there, the fire jumped north and east, igniting the roof of Otto Duker's Box Factory near Eastern Avenue and Albemarle Street. Firefighters extinguished both blazes, preventing the fire from gaining a foothold east of the falls. Next, New Yorkers fought the fire at the Maine Lake Ice Company near Philpot and Thames Streets. Howe then sent Engine Companies 5 and 27 to Francis Denmead's Malt House at the foot of President Street with orders to keep it from catching fire, since burning malt particles could rise into the air, travel downwind, and shower communities east of the falls with sparks. Moving east toward the Jones Falls, the New Yorkers became part of a major effort to stop the fire at this seventy-five-foot-wide, north-south waterway. The second trainload of New Yorkers arrived in Baltimore shortly after 3 P.M. Monday and linked up with their colleagues. Though sometimes unable to see through the dense smoke, the New Yorkers nevertheless stood their ground. Reinforcements soon arrived from other fire departments and it became a battle of the cities against the raging fire. Before long, Baltimore stood shoulder to shoulder with New York, Washington, Philadelphia, Chester,

and York. Howe deployed some of his firefighters to the Savannah Pier, located near Block Street and West Falls Avenue, where the New Yorkers and others successfully controlled the fire in this particular area.

The arrival of reinforcements made possible a stronger concentration of men along the Jones Falls. Determined to stop the fire there, they extinguished small fires that had started on the east side of the waterway, while directing hoses at buildings on the west side. Sporadic fires continued to start west of the falls. The storage shed of the American Ice Company on West Falls Avenue was the last building to erupt into a blaze, and it was New York companies who fought it there. Fires that had previously raged now lessened in intensity as they consumed nearby buildings, using up their sources of fuel. Additional firefighters who had completed much of their work in other parts of the fire zone now joined those on the southeast corner. Their combined efforts finally brought the fire under control about 5 P.M. on Monday. As the sun began to set, Howe searched for, and found, Emrich. "I have the honor to report that your fire is under control," he said.[30]

Although Howe had expected to leave Baltimore around ten on Tuesday morning, Baltimore officials persuaded him to remain a few more hours to help allay the fears of many Baltimoreans that not enough firefighters were available to confront the still-smoldering fire in the event it burst out of control again. Howe and his men eventually left Baltimore just before 2 P.M. on Tuesday, departing from Camden Street Station. On the train Chief Howe recounted for reporters some of the vivid and bizarre scenes his men had witnessed during the blaze. He also mentioned the kindness they received from the employees of the Merchants and Miners'

Transportation Company, who had given them food and hot coffee at a time when they needed it most.[31]

All during the New Yorkers' tough assignment in Baltimore, a stray dog had accompanied Engine Company No. 26, often giving the impression that it was guiding the horses as they pulled their engine from blaze to blaze. Although he responded to the name "Jack," the firefighters named him "Baltimore." As their train prepared to depart for New York, the dog stood by, looking on wistfully. One firefighter impulsively grabbed him and hoisted him onto the train. As the New Yorkers slowly pulled away from the station for the ride home, a crowd of thankful Baltimoreans cheered them and handed up flasks of bourbon and rye and boxes of cigars. Engine Company No. 26's John Kelly acted as the master of ceremonies, officially naming their new mascot "Baltimore" by pouring whiskey over his head and declaring, "I christen thee Baltimore." The worn-out men cheered huskily.[32]

New York Fire Commissioner Nicholas J. Hayes and Fire Chief Edward F. Croker rushed to the Jersey City ferry terminal to greet their returning firemen. Although it took considerable effort to unload the engines, the horses alighted easily, as they had become accustomed to getting in and out of boxcars. As the firefighters, covered with dirt and soot, hungry and tired, stood in the rail yards, Chief Howe took a fancy to the new company mascot but viewed its future with poignant pessimism. "He will meet the fate of fire dogs. He will have a grand time until he gets old, loses his hearing, and is run over by an engine or truck. That's the way they go," the chief sighed as he glanced sadly down at the dog.[33] Moving on to the ferry terminal, Commissioner Hayes addressed the firefight-

ers in the waiting room as they ate sandwiches and drank hot coffee.

Engine Companies Nos. 5, 16, and 26 boarded the ferry that would take them to the foot of Twenty-third Street in Manhattan, nearest to their station houses. As the men from Engine No. 26 began to board the ferry, Baltimore ran ahead of the horses, and ferry attendants attempted to chase him off the boat. The company raised a shout, and two men, ready to fight, jumped off the engine, bellowing, "Let Baltimore alone!" They rescued him and went on their way to the Twenty-third Street ferry slip. More than a thousand New Yorkers greeted them at the ferry gate, wildly shouting, "Three cheers for the New York Fire Department!" The companies rode off the ferry on their horse-drawn equipment, ringing their bells and disturbing the sleep of some for about half a mile. Crowds cheered the three companies all along Twenty-third Street. At another landing, Engine Company No. 5 traveled to their firehouse on Fourteenth Street as enthusiastic New Yorkers cheered them all along the way. Engine Companies Nos. 7 and 12 crossed the Hudson on the Cortlandt Street Ferry. When they landed in Manhattan, hundreds of well-wishers also greeted them. Policemen doffed their helmets in salute. At their station houses the men cleaned up their gear and went home for the night. When they reported for duty at eight the next morning, they discovered a two-day leave of absence awaiting them.[34]

On Saturday, February 13, five days after the fire, several of the reporters who had accompanied New York's firefighters to Baltimore stopped by Engine Company No. 26 to visit with the men and their heroic mascot. Not recognizing the reporters, Baltimore hid behind his firefighting friends with teeth bared and hair bristling along his spine until convinced they were friendly. The reporters presented Baltimore with a collar decorated with large brass studs and bearing a plate inscribed, "Baltimore, February 9, 1904, A Waif From the Flames." Strutting by the horses in his new collar, Baltimore wagged his stub of a tail, showing them that he, too, wore a harness.[35]

As Baltimore became accustomed to his new home, the members of Engine Company No. 26 described him as a "foxhound or if he ain't that, he is a breed all to himself." Indeed, finding the proper food for Baltimore seemed difficult; he would not eat much of anything except a few scraps of ham. Puzzled, the firefighters thought he must be a sea dog, accustomed to eating oysters, as sea dogs might do in a city like Baltimore. A neighbor came to Baltimore's rescue by suggesting dog biscuits. "Baltimore took to them like a child to ice cream," said a firefighter. "Whoever formerly owned him must have been an aristocrat."[36]

ATLANTIC CITY
— "The Last Hurrah"

The big city units might have had the largest impact on extinguishing the Great Baltimore Fire, but far smaller companies had much to be proud of in their effort. The Great Fire became the last hurrah for Atlantic City's brave volunteers from the seashore, a contingent of seventy-eight firemen and fourteen ordinary citizens. Less than two months after their participation in the fight against Baltimore's blaze, a paid Atlantic City fire department replaced this volunteer unit. Yet, the volunteers certainly concluded their service with spirit. While they did not bring any apparatus, they fought alongside professional firefighters from the big cities. In addition to

Atlantic City's enthusiastic amateurs, other volunteer units included Marylanders from Sparrows Point, Relay, and St. Denis.

On Monday morning, the increasingly worried McLane sent a telegram to Atlantic City mayor Franklin P. Stoy stating that Baltimore's firefighters "had been on the fire lines for nearly 24 hours and were near complete exhaustion and replacements were needed immediately."[37] Stoy contacted Atlantic City Fire Chief Isaac Wiesenthal, who issued a call for volunteers to every fire station in the city. Concurrently, Stoy arranged for rail transportation with the West Jersey and Seashore Railroad at a cost, records show, of $200.85. Many Atlantic City volunteer firefighters already knew of the fire, while others quickly learned about it. A signal sounded just after 11 A.M., rallying about 125 volunteers to assemble at the railroad station. Doctors examined the volunteers and selected the seventy-eight fittest to board the train for Baltimore, along with fourteen hardy citizens. The youngest of the volunteers, Earl Battinger, sixteen, replaced his father, Harry J. Battinger, who was unavailable for the trip. Earl took his father's boots, coat, and helmet and reported with the other volunteers at the station. Although initially rejected by those selecting the volunteers to go, young Battinger's enthusiasm, stature, and strength eventually won out. Two physicians and one dentist were among the fourteen citizens that accompanied the firefighters. The physicians would treat the injured and observe the firefighters, ordering exhausted men off the fire lines. After speeding along the salt marshes of New Jersey, the train passed Haddonfield traveling sixty miles per hour. Bypassing the Broad Street Station in Philadelphia, the Atlantic City firefighters made the 155-mile trip to Baltimore in four hours.

When they arrived they raced to City Hall and volunteered for the most difficult tasks. Quickly dispatched to the southeast portion of the fire zone, Atlantic City firemen contributed to Monday afternoon's major campaigns to stop the fire from crossing the Jones Falls and halt its progress toward the docks to the south. In fighting the fire at the lumberyards near the Jones Falls, they relieved weary Philadelphians and companies from Altoona. In addition, several Atlantic City companies were among those attempting to block the fire at the Jones Falls and along President Street. As fires were contained Monday afternoon, Atlantic City volunteers were assigned to squads of ten men, each led by one of their more experienced firefighters, and sent off to other locations as needed. Several squads fought more fires in the lumberyard district while others took up positions along the Jones Falls. One hastily dispatched squad battled a fire adjacent to the basin.

The Atlantic City volunteers also stood side by side with New York and Philadelphia professionals as they fought the fire at the wharf of the Merchants and Miners' Transportation Company, located at West Falls Avenue and Block Street. Although their fire lines bent from time to time, they never broke. Near the end, they also helped fight the fire at the American Ice Company. Atlantic City volunteer firefighting lore includes a story told by Fred C. Muller, a member of the Chelsea Fire Company No. 6, that "each explosion in a canning factory showered the men with apples." On Monday night, temperatures again dropped below freezing and many of the men stood in a mixture of water and ice. Adelbert Driscoll and a group of firefighters from the Neptune Hose Company No. 1 repaid a nearly two-year-old debt to Philadelphia Engine Company No. 43, which had raced to Atlantic City to help fight Atlantic City's Great Boardwalk Fire of April 3, 1902. The Atlantic City firefighters moved in to relieve their exhausted, one-time saviors, much to the Pennsylvanians' delight.

On Tuesday morning, February 9, Mayor Stoy received a telegram from Louis H. Donnelly, fire commissioner of the Atlantic City volunteers who was with the men in Baltimore. "Fire under control. Atlantic City boys did good work. Will leave here at 11:00 A.M. All alive." Crowds cheered in Baltimore as the Atlantic City volunteers departed. When they returned home late Tuesday afternoon, a citizen's committee and a brass band met them beneath a large banner declaring, "We Hazard Our All." Although no one from Atlantic City received a serious injury, rumors circulated that William J. Black in the Neptune Hose Company was losing his eyesight because of injuries received in Baltimore. He quickly stopped a Baltimore fundraising committee when he learned about its efforts. "I feel as happy as a clam at high tide," Black told his would-be benefactors, explaining that he had gotten some ashes in his eyes but had recovered.[38] That evening, Stoy hosted a dinner in honor of the firefighters in Atlantic City's Hygeia Hotel. New York Fire Commissioner Nicholas J. Hayes presented Stoy with a gold replica of a fire engine for his watch chain in honor of the Atlantic City volunteer fire department's outstanding work.

Photograph of an injured firefighter. The man is possibly George W. Gail, Jr., president of the Board of Fire Commissioners. MdHS

3

Call Out the Troops

PON LEARNING THAT
Washington had dispatched firefighters to help Baltimore battle its
terrifying blaze, President Theodore
Roosevelt stepped in to aid the capital's
beleaguered neighbor to the north. As a former New York City police commissioner,
Roosevelt naturally turned to the cops. He
contacted the District of Columbia's police
chief, Major Richard Sylvester, and directed
him "to render all the assistance he could" to
Baltimore. Sylvester dispatched Captain Isaac
Pearson with a detail of thirty policemen to
Baltimore to help preserve order there.[1]
Although detectives and out-of-town patrolmen proved useful in reinforcing the
Baltimore Police Department, the problem
was not fighting crime or preventing looting
but crowd control. As the fire zone expanded,
officials needed hundreds of police officers to
cordon off and handle the thousands of spectators forming in increasing numbers, particularly after the spectacular smoke explosion
shattered the Sunday morning calm.
Spectators breaching the fire line endangered
themselves and interfered with firefighters.

Mayor McLane appeared to have control
of the crisis at its start. Cool under pressure
and decisive, McLane seemed to be the right
man at the right place. Yet as he became more
involved in choosing strategies for fighting the
fire, a role he was not equipped to fill,
McLane made some disastrous decisions. With
Chief Horton's injury and evacuation from
the fire scene, McLane found himself working
with August Emrich, a less experienced leader
of firefighters. The mayor was instrumental in
ordering the dynamiting of buildings to stem
the fire's advance, a tactic that a seasoned fire
chief like Horton would not have undertaken.
On the other hand, his decision to call for the
help of state troops proved sound. Unfortu-
ately, politics would cloud the situation and
initially obscure the chain of command.

Unlike asking another mayor for help in
the event of a fire, McLane faced a more
complicated situation when seeking assistance
from the Maryland National Guard. The key
issue involved control. With the state's adjutant
general in charge of the Guard, one could
argue that he should have commanded the
troops, but that was not the case during the
Baltimore Fire. In an 1896 statute, the
Maryland legislature had provided that in
cases of civil emergency the local civilian
authority could control the Guard. While
McLane agreed with the need to request
assistance from the Maryland National Guard,

FACING PAGE:
Soldiers man the cordon
at 16 East Lexington
Street. An officer with
drawn sabre glares at
spectators standing
behind the cordon.
Maryland State Archives

National Guardsmen man the cordon of the Burnt District, restraining an apparently cooperative crowd of spectators. MdHS

the law stipulated that this request had to come from the Baltimore Board of Police Commissioners. The Maryland National Guard had not been called into action since the railroad strike of 1877.[2]

The law gave the Board of Police Commissioners the authority to call out the National Guard to help quell civil disruption or suppress riots, and only the governor could countermand the board's orders.[3] That left the state's adjutant general, Clinton L. Riggs, brother of Brigadier General Lawrason Riggs, on the outside looking in. Consequently, around 5:30 P.M. on Sunday, as the fire raged, the Guard's senior military officer, General Riggs, did not report to his brother the adjutant general but to the Baltimore Board of Police Commissioners, in a meeting with George M. Upshur, president of the board. Citing the state militia law, Upshur ordered Riggs to have the Baltimore-based Fourth and Fifth Regiments of the Guard surround the fire area, keep the public away from it,

and prevent looting. Immediately following this meeting in Baltimore, Riggs attempted to call Annapolis to speak to Governor Warfield. He wanted to be certain that the governor agreed with Upshur's action to take over direction of the Guard, and make sure that Upshur's plans did not interfere with anything the governor had in mind. Unable to get Warfield on the line, Riggs eventually decided to follow Upshur's orders. At 7:30 P.M., two hours after the start of his meeting with Upshur, Riggs directed the regimental commanders to assemble and outfit companies of twenty men. These units were to report to him at brigade headquarters at Fayette and Calvert Streets, a block west of City Hall, where Riggs had his command post in the Police Board offices in the courthouse.[4]

The Guard was slow to respond. Members of the Fourth and Fifth Regiments who did report quickly for duty discovered their armories locked up tight and no way to get in. Members of the Fourth Regiment climbed onto the roof of the building adjoining their West Fayette Street armory in order to gain entrance, while Fifth Regiment guardsmen had to wait for the commander of their armory on North Howard Street to show up around 8 P.M. with a key. The first guardsmen to gain entry to their armories encountered locked supply and arms rooms. In many cases, they just had to break into these areas. Difficulties also surfaced in rounding up sufficient forces. Unable to contact many other National Guardsmen by telephone or telegraph, Riggs's men tried two less sophisticated approaches: running through the city and knocking on doors to call out their comrades, and sounding a general alarm, using the large bell in the cupola atop the City Hall dome. Those who tried to locate fellow guardsmen by running door-to-door had little success. The City Hall bell proved

far more effective. Lieutenant Colonel J. Frank Supplee, Executive Officer of the Fourth Regiment, sent one of his men to ask McLane to authorize the sounding of riot call on the City Hall bell. Surprised by the request, McLane telephoned Supplee for clarification. Supplee explained that a well-established, prearranged signal for a riot call involved ringing the bell, three series of three tolls, about six times, whereupon McLane reportedly climbed up to the belfry and rang the bell himself.[5] Ringing the riot call alerted many of the troops, who began assembling at their regimental headquarters. Although Riggs received his directions to call out the Guard at 5:30 P.M., it was not until 9 P.M. that McLane sounded the riot call and sizable numbers of troops started to form.

Riggs divided his operational sector in two. He ordered the Fourth Regiment to

Members of the Maryland National Guard's First Regiment pose before their mess tent at Fayette Street west of Gay Street. These men were reportedly from Annapolis.
MdHS

Turmoil at the Labor Lyceum

AT THE TIME OF THE GREAT FIRE, Baltimore shared America's affinity for naming institutions after the fashion of ancient Greece. Both labor and management joined in this practice. Four blocks north of the fire zone, the affluent drank and dined at the Athenaeum Club. Three blocks east of the fire zone, a union hall named the Labor Lyceum stood on East Baltimore Street.

While the more well-heeled National Guardsmen, generally members of the cavalry troop, enjoyed meals at the posh Athenaeum Club, the Labor Lyceum that the Guard temporarily rented for its rank-and-file held no particular charms for the more than four hundred guardsmen from the Fifth Regiment who crammed into it from February 8 to February 23. Posted on guard duty outside in frigid weather, the men brought into their temporary barracks wintertime coughing and sneezing all too common in the conditions they endured. In the confined sleeping spaces, this led to numerous respiratory ailments, infections, and general misery.

Some of the soldiers vented their wrath at the wretched conditions on the building when they moved out. Max Quith, Secretary of the Labor Lyceum Association, submitted an angry complaint for restitution to Brigadier General Riggs on April 7, 1904, along with a claim for $341.30.[1] Quith complained that the troops "seemed to take pleasure in breaking windows, electric light bulbs, and chairs."[2] Worse, overflowing wastewater on the second floor had destroyed twenty yards of ceiling plaster on the first floor. The cause appeared to be a clogged sink and urinal, stopped up with remnants of the men's dinner. In another room, an overflowing waste box in the main hall, choked with beans, ruined plaster around the doorframe and ceiling.[3]

The cavalry, in unsurprising contrast, were evidently content with the refined meals and elegant surroundings of the Athenaeum Club.

---

[1] Enclosure #1 to 1st endorsement on claim #5857. Headquarters, First Brigade, Maryland National Guard, April 8, 1904.

[2] Letter, Labor Lyceum Association, Baltimore, Md. April 7, 1904, p. 1, Max Quith, Secretary of the Labor Lyceum Association. Letter to 1st Brigade Commanding General, Maryland National Guard.

[3] Itemized claim attached to letter dated April 7, 1904 from Max Quith to Commanding General 1st Brigade.

Labor Lyceum, 1011 E. Baltimore Street, three blocks east of the Jones Falls. MdHS

A platoon of Fifth Regiment guardsmen crosses the East Baltimore Street Bridge over the Jones Falls. The Monumental Bowling Alley behind them was a center of the relatively new Maryland sport of "duckpin" bowling. Maryland State Archives.

secure the area west of Calvert Street while the Fifth secured the area east of it. Saratoga Street formed the northern boundary of Guard operations, the harbor basin the southern boundary. Riggs ordered both regiments to clear their areas of civilians ahead of the flames.

Even this simple plan proved slow in starting because regimental commanders had difficulty assembling their units. Most officers and enlisted men in the Guard either were watching the fire or helping evacuate and safeguard moveable assets threatened by it. The first company with enough men to deploy left the Fourth Regiment's armory by 9 P.M. It consisted of thirteen enlisted men, commanded by Captain Bruce B. Gootee.

When Gootee reported to Riggs, the general gave him uncomplicated but specific instructions: "Keep the crowd back as the fire approaches."[6] How Gootee should go about it was unclear. Handling potentially uncooperative spectators was not something for which guardsmen train. Riggs simply told Gootee to use his own judgment. Gootee and his troops then reported to Police Marshal Thomas F. Farnan at South and Baltimore Streets, and as additional units from the Fourth Regiment became available, Riggs posted them so they would form a cordon on the north and west sides of the fire. By midnight, the cordon extended all the way to Pratt and Howard Streets.

Untrained in crowd control, the men of
the Fourth Regiment did their best to hold
back the growing horde of spectators by sta-
tioning themselves on a picket line between a
large group of civilians to their front and the
intensifying blaze behind them. Numerous
citizens tried to penetrate the regiment's lines
and determine the extent of the damage
inflicted on their businesses or just see what
was happening. When crowds pushed against
their lines, the soldiers held their rifles at
"Port Arms," diagonally across their chests,
and pushed back. But the crowd could not
help but notice that they had also fixed bayonets, and although these were for the moment
pointed up and to the side rather than at the
crowd, there was little doubt in anyone's mind
that that could quickly change. Lieutenant
Colonel Supplee emphasized the point by

drawing his ceremonial sword and assisting
"his men by forcing the crowd back with the
flat of the blade," according to subsequent
accounts.7 Unlike the Fourth, the Fifth
Regiment, stationed on the east side of the
cordon, faced a fire bearing down on them as
they attempted to evacuate all civilians from
buildings and streets. The first company
deployed from the Fifth Regiment, commanded by Captain Washington Bowie Jr.,
arrived at brigade headquarters at 9:50 P.M.
This company consisted of Bowie and thirty
men who were early arrivals from four other
companies. Now ready for deployment,
Captain Bowie moved quickly with his composite company to South and Water Streets to
clear all civilians from the area as flames
approached from the northwest and north. In
fact, Bowie's unit was the only company from

the slow forming Fifth Regiment available for clearing about twelve blocks between Water and Pratt Streets from Light Street to the Jones Falls. Bowie's company also attempted to clear the wharves and waterfront area.

Some of the more spirited encounters occurred when members of Bowie's unit attempted to eject drunks from bars in the path of the fire. It was clear that the fire would eventually destroy the saloons, but

Mounted First Brigade officer making the rounds and inspecting the guard. Maryland State Archives

some imbibers deemed it shameful to let good whiskey go to waste. In some instances, Bowie later reported, "drunken men had been enticed to saloons where free drinks were being dispensed." Lieutenant S. E. Conradt recalled "having to break into a burning hotel at the corner of Pratt and West Falls Streets to eject about a dozen men." He reasoned that "the patrons were saving it [fine liquor] in the most approved fashion." At the same saloon, according to an official report, guardsmen "discovered another man on the building's roof holding a single bucket of water." When the man refused to move, troops carried him out of harm's way. The hotel, according to Conradt, "burned to the ground within thirty minutes."[8]

Riggs's First Brigade labored through most of the night without rest. As the winds shifted after midnight, blowing the fire to the east, firefighters and guardsmen joined forces to form a barrier against the blaze at the Jones Falls and hold back civilians east of that waterway. To be effective, firefighters had to

Guard tent at Liberty and Howard Streets. MdHS

Maryland National Guardsmen in the street beside a steam engine used for pulling down buildings. MdHS

man this potential natural barrier with well-positioned fire engines, and they had to be free from crowds of spectators. The line of defense included firefighters from many out-of-town units as well. Finally, after numerous delays and changes in direction, all these units merged. Guardsmen in both regimental areas helped firemen by driving back crowds and making way for horse-drawn fire engines to shift positions and stay ahead of the fire. Other troops evacuated any citizens still on the west side of the Jones Falls. Guardsmen

near the falls continued to scour saloons and hotels for drunks, "at least one of whom had to be carried by guardsmen across a bridge." Patrons of one saloon on Albemarle Street defied attempts to vacate the place by locking themselves inside despite the fire moving in their direction. The battalion commander of a Guard unit, Major John Hinkley, "ordered . . . [the door] broken down and then ejected all of the bar's occupants."9

After evacuating most of the civilians from the west side of the Jones Falls, the

Guard and firemen concentrated on stopping the fire there at the falls. Fifth Regiment commander Colonel Henry M. Warfield, a distant cousin of the governor, ordered Hinkley's battalion now to fight the fire. Troops from Hinkley's battalion began with the lumberyards along the lower end of East Falls Avenue, in one instance throwing a small stack of lumber into the Jones Falls to prevent it from igniting.[10]

As more men gathered in the southeast corner of the fire zone, Hinkley attempted to relieve his men for breakfast, but the fire allowed no time for luxury. Half the men got nothing at all, though two of Hinkley's companies had received food earlier from civilians. At about the same time, guardsmen in the Fourth Regiment, deployed on the less active west side picket line had "hot coffee, hot sausage and bread" distributed to them from a borrowed hose wagon.[11]

Although the Fifth Regiment battled the fire continuously in the southeast until it was brought under control, the fire in the Fourth Regiment's area subsided sufficiently to enable many units to adopt a rotation of four-hours-on/eight-hours-off duty. Much work still remained to be done. Riggs estimated that it would take far more troops than he had on hand to cordon off the smoldering burnt district. On Monday he decided to activate additional units from around the state. All that afternoon and evening, First Regiment guardsmen from Annapolis, Bel Air, Cambridge, Centreville, Cumberland, Easton, Elkton, Hagerstown, Rockville, Salisbury, and Westminster boarded trains for Baltimore.[12] Arriving in the city, these units marched to the Fifth Regiment's armory and formed into three battalions of four companies each. The plan for their deployment included a rotation whereby two battalions

would man the cordon while one battalion rested.

Among the National Guard's First Brigade was Cavalry Troop A, out of Pikesville under the command of Captain Joseph W. Shirley. These were for the most part men of means employed mainly in white-collar professions. Each could and did provide his own horse. One of the troopers, Corporal Robert Garrett, grandson of a former B&O president and winner of gold medals in shot put and discus for the United States' 1896 Olympic team, was described in the *Baltimore American* as "one of the wealthiest and most prominent young men in Baltimore."[13]

After the fire had been brought under control, the cavalry patrolled the streets near

In addition to manning the cordon surrounding the Burnt District Maryland National Guard soldiers and sailors patrol the interior. Sailors, unlike the soldiers seem to be wamly dressed. The steam engine at right was used to pull down walls. Maryland State Archives

Guardsmen and their makeshift shelter at Liberty and Baltimore Streets. MdHS

buildings set for demolition and drove off anyone approaching these dangerous places. Since demolition crews used dynamite only during the day, the cavalry slept comfortably at night in the vacated nurses' quarters in City Hospital, two blocks north of the fire zone at Calvert and Pleasant Streets, and took many of their meals at the Athenaeum Club at 2 East Franklin Street, four blocks north of the

fire zone. As might be expected, they looked dashing in their uniforms and carried themselves accordingly.

Riggs also activated the Naval Brigade to guard Baltimore's waterfront, and a Signal Corps unit to provide communications within the military forces. Since the eight-man Signal Corps contingent arrived without any equipment, the Maryland Telephone Company had to provide it. Navy guardsmen suffered under some of the harshest conditions, enduring wind and biting cold while patrolling the water and working on open wharves. Headquartered on the U.S.S. *Sylvia*, moored at Bowley's Wharf at the foot of Franklin Lane east of Cheapside, these sailors patrolled the harbor day and night, maintaining the southern portion of the cordon and keeping away waterborne spectators. The naval contingent never constituted more than 142 men and averaged 134 until George Upshur, president of the Board of Police Commissioners, dismissed them on February 23.[14]

On the second day of the fire, officials from state, city, and military organizations realized they had to modify and clarify the policy of excluding all civilians from the fire zone. At first, they had issued signed entry passes to the area, but difficulties quickly arose when numerous passes appeared, issued from many sources, including the mayor's office, the police commissioner's office, the governor's office, and officers of the First Brigade. Inconsistent procedures adopted by various Guard units in honoring these passes added to the confusion. As a result, state, city, and military representatives met the next day, Tuesday,

Soldiers and sailors pose before City Hall. MdHS

Northern District policemen. MdHS

February 9, and attempted to find a way to secure the Burnt District and at the same time permit entry to those whose situation required it. They made the Board of Police Commissioners the sole authority for approving the passes. Riggs, who was responsible for the security of the Burnt District, issued them.[15] Upshur and Riggs adopted this procedure in the hope that it would prevent looting and avoid injury by excluding "pedestrians."

The solution satisfied practically no one. Prominent businessmen and news reporters were outraged when the board refused them passes, and Riggs rapidly became the target of their wrath. The *Baltimore Sun* reacted to its reporters' exclusion from the fire zone by tartly observing that Baltimoreans "could get along without the militia better than they could without newspapers." By withholding passes, Riggs "doubled the already difficult work of newspaper men," the *Sun* complained. The *Annapolis Evening Capital*

seethed, "Would not Generalissimo Riggs feel pretty bad if there were no newspapers to report his greatness?" Riggs initially refused to budge, but "after McLane intervened, the general agreed to issue five passes to each newspaper."[16] No sooner had he done so than reporters objected to the limit of five passes per paper. Out-of-town reporters, to whom the board also denied entrance, described Baltimore as a dictatorship. One *Philadelphia Inquirer* article, headlined "Under Military Rule," proclaimed, "The city has been, and still is, under quasi-military rule." Other journalists proved less pugnacious. One corrected an "erroneous report [that] stated Baltimore had been placed under martial law." Riggs tried to assure one reporter that "the soldiers were simply assisting the police to maintain order and guard the burned district."[17] His statement, although correct, angered reporters who had been denied passes or restricted in any way by the military, and they remained outspoken in their displeasure during the seventeen days the military served in Baltimore.

With Riggs reporting to Baltimore's Board of Police Commissioners, McLane had the luxury of control without having to take such criticism. Governor Warfield also escaped the anger, even though he seemed far more focused on maintaining the security of the Fidelity Deposit & Trust Company, the pioneering surety bonding firm he had founded and of which he continued as president, than on overseeing the salvation of Baltimore. Warfield had arrived in Baltimore from Annapolis late in the evening on the first day of the fire and immediately set up his executive headquarters in his Fidelity office, where he remained throughout the crisis. Warfield even ordered the sentries on the cordon near Saratoga and Charles Streets one block north of the Fidelity & Deposit Company to "allow only those having business in the Fidelity building to pass."[18] Although Warfield had complained about being unable to make contact with Fidelity after repeated calls during the first day of the fire, in turn he was unavailable to receive Riggs's calls about the deployment of the National Guard in Baltimore. Warfield, who clearly considered the creation of the Fidelity & Deposit Company his finest accomplishment, would later direct his epitaph to read: "Founder of the Fidelity and Deposit Company and Governor of Maryland," in that order.[19]

After the blaze was brought under control Monday night, the troops on the cordon were as exhausted, cold, and hungry as the firefighters themselves. Replaced on the line by other troops for a few hours, they slept when they could and cleaned up. Augmenting their cordon around the burnt district was an interior roving patrol to apprehend any looters who might penetrate the barriers. The Signal Corps laid communications wires

between units, and Riggs's military force settled into a more routine period of guard duty. It would have been dull but for the nature of their uniforms, which though adequate for walking briefly in the cold were hardly suited for remaining out-of-doors for an extended period in blustery, icy weather. After prolonged exposure to these harsh elements, two men in the Fourth Regiment died of pneumonia. Both became ill while stationed in Baltimore and died after their commanders sent them home. Second Lieutenant John V. Richardson of Company E died on February 17, and Private John Undutch from Company F on February 21.

On February 22, Governor Warfield wrote to Adjutant General Clinton L. Riggs, "The time has arrived for the withdrawal of the militia." Forwarded to the president of the Board of Police Commissioners, the gover-

A National Guard wagon at the southeast corner of Gay and Lombard Streets waits to carry guardsmen to their posts. MdHS

79

nor's assessment generated a speedy response.
George Upshur relieved the remaining units
of the First Brigade effective February 23 at 6
P.M.[20]

The Maryland National Guard had provided a degree of order to what otherwise
might have been chaos for Baltimore. After
service in the Spanish-American War six years
earlier, some veterans who joined the Guard
tended to concentrate on parades rather than
soldiering in the field and seemed more inter-
ested in the social trappings associated with
the notion that "rank has its privileges."
Despite delays in getting started, poor equipment, inadequate uniforms, and uncertain
command arrangements though, the Guard
deployed effectively. It also probably benefited
from the experience, learning lessons in readiness and public relations with business and
the press.

4

Stop it at the Jones Falls

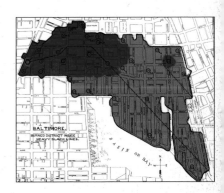

THE FIRE CONTINUED at a brisk pace into Monday. Many of the firefighters, policemen, city employees, soldiers, and sailors who had worked all night were groggy long before dawn. Firefighters in particular appeared to be tired, wet, dirty, bruised, and stretched emotionally. Many suffered from aching legs and feet after standing most of the night, sometimes in ice and blackened slush. Eyes swelled from smoke irritation. Those helping the firefighters— medical personnel, railroad workers, and restaurant staffs—also faced exhaustion.

Many spectators, especially those with more than a passing interest in the fire, also stayed up all night. Some had homes or businesses in the path of the advancing flames. In addition to the roofs or windows of houses, popular vantage points included nearby Federal Hill across the harbor basin just south of the fire, as well as the more distant hills of Highland Town to the east and the high ground of Druid Hill Park to the north. The roofs of tall buildings were soon crowded with spectators. The new Belvedere Hotel, completed less than two months earlier eleven blocks north of the fire zone on Chase Street, became an especially popular observation post. Many who watched the fire devouring

their city prayed that the fire would spare their homes. Prayer and worry also mounted in the countryside, for many there did not yet know the cause of the spectral glow on the horizon.

Family members and strangers brought food and coffee to the embattled firefighters and policemen. Sometimes a fireman's wife appeared at the edge of the fire zone, carrying her husband's dinner pail. One declared, "I bring him his supper every night and he needs to have something to eat." Others stood beside the laboring firefighters and fed them by hand, since the men needed both of their own to aim the hoses on the flames. The military fed their troops. Lunch counters and restaurants remained open all night, with a few providing free food and coffee to their friends and regular customers. Other establishments near the edge of the fire zone did a profitable business selling sandwiches and coffee to those who lingered on throughout the night. Some went home and returned with blankets, food, coffee, and water for those family members who had remained at the fire scene. The station house for Engine Company No. 6, located at Gay and Ensor Streets, served as an emergency hospital. Doctors and nurses treated more than 150 firefighters for a wide

FACING PAGE:
Sunday evening the wind shifted, blowing from the west, then northwest. Here the printing firm of Guggenheimer, Weil, and Company, on the northeast corner of Liberty and Lombard Streets and containing volatile printing chemicals, is in flames. By midnight, the fire had swept first northeast, then east, then southeast, nearly tripling the area of destruction. MdHS

City Hall illuminated by the flames. The photograph was taken at 1:30 Monday morning from Mercy Hospital. MdHS

range of injuries and burns, none of them life threatening.[1]

Care and feeding was not limited to persons. People from all occupations tended to the hundreds of fire department, police, and military horses needing food, water, and on a few occasions, blankets. Like their human counterparts, the horses also suffered from overwork and exhaustion. The fire departments, the Baltimore Police Department, Cavalry Troop A from the Maryland National Guard, and the army garrison at Fort McHenry pooled their resources to care for all the horses in the vicinity. Considerable sharing of hay, oats, and assistance in the repair of harnesses and rigging took place, particu-

The Post Office Building,
also photographed from
Mercy Hospital. MdHS

larly in support of the horses belonging to out-of-town fire departments.

Many Baltimore families whose homes lay in the fire's path put their children to bed fully dressed so they would be ready if they had to evacuate quickly. They took turns watching for the advancing fire, packed their valuables in manageable loads that could be moved at a moment's notice, and remained alert lest sparks or embers might land on or near their houses. Those who lived on the eastern side of the Jones Falls hoped that this slender waterway, only seventy-five feet wide, would stop the advancing fire. The increasing strength of the wind from the northwest intensified the flames at the Maryland

The Church of the Messiah, on the southwest corner of Fayette and Gay Streets, was the only church destroyed in the fire. This photograph was taken about 1 o'clock Monday morning, the light being the glow of the fire. The bell of the church fell down through the tower, and the photographer might have tripped his shutter at precisely that instant. MdHS See detail on page 87.

Institute in Centre Market Space at Baltimore Street, bringing the fire perilously close to the falls. People residing near the institute fled to the eastern side of the falls, and for a time the flames seemed to chase them.

Since the fire had destroyed the Western Union Office in the Equitable Building and the Associated Press offices in the Herald Building, both telegraphers and newsmen needed a new communications center. At 2 A.M., Monday, the Western Union keymen began transmitting their messages from Martin J. Welsh's House of Welsh restaurant and saloon on the northeast corner of Saratoga Street and Guilford Avenue. The

telegraphers set up in a small room directly under the restaurant's roof, reached by climbing a narrow side stairway. Although it had been closed by the mayor along with the rest of the city's saloons, the House of Welsh had the good fortune to be located next to what was reportedly the only unburned telegraph pole with undamaged lines in Baltimore. With no financial reward, Martin Welsh rallied to the cause, and for the next seventy-two hours his place served as Baltimore's telegraph outlet to the world.[2]

Although safe from the flames in her family's three-story rowhouse with a little white stoop at 329 North Carrollton Avenue,

Enlarged detail
from facing page.

eight-year-old Rosa Kohler still did not know how or where her parents were. Her grandfather owned a shoe factory on Water Street, as well as three retail shoe stores. The factory and a store in the Sun Building at Charles and Baltimore Streets burned. During the night, while Rosa's father, a Western Union telegrapher, set off to help set up the transmission office in the attic of Welsh's Restaurant and Saloon, her mother seemingly disappeared. Frantic about her parents' absence, Rosa did not see either until early Monday morning when her mother returned home and explained that she had spent the night with a friend on Biddle Street, helping

her pack and prepare to move in case the wind shifted. She also described how she had miraculously encountered Rosa's father. Both had gone to inspect her grandfather's shoe factory, and had met in its ruins.[3]

During the night, Joseph L. Wickes, Baltimore's Commissioner of Street Cleaning, had assembled a group of workers under supervisor Edward F. Callahan, Superintendent of the Second District, to help prevent the fire from spreading to City Hall. Provided with buckets of water, these men patrolled the roof and dome of City Hall to extinguish falling sparks and roamed the building to ensure that all windows remained closed. On Monday

Church of the Messiah
in ruins. MdHS

morning, after the fire no longer threatened City Hall, this force of street cleaners assembled and offered their services to the Baltimore fire department. Assigned temporarily to handle the hoses, the street cleaners doused the flames while the firemen rested and ate breakfast.[4]

As the second day of the fire began, the blaze advanced southward toward Pratt Street. As it ignited several buildings near Pratt, sailors manning ships on the northern side of the Baltimore basin grew increasingly worried about the safety of their vessels, many of them with flammable rigging and wooden hulls. As the flames moved closer to their ships and barges, the captains all reached the same conclusion about the same time and tried to sail

away from the Pratt Street docks toward safety on the opposite side of the basin. Tugs moving swiftly from the southern side to rescue barges moored below Pratt Street added to the confusion. The congested mass of tugs, barges, steamers, and bay schooners looked to some observers like a maritime stampede.

From the fire's first hours, boats and ships in the harbor had tried to assist those battling the flames on shore, and their efforts never ceased. Vivian Phillips, captain of the tugboat *Oriole*, heard shouts for help early Sunday morning from the flour mill of the C. A. Gambrill Manufacturing Company. Easing his way in to Smith's dock at the foot of Gay Street, he noticed that flames advancing from Pratt Street had trapped five men who had

been drinking wine and spending the night on the portion of the mill next to the water's edge. Phillips rescued the men and transferred them to a police boat. By midnight, he sent the *Oriole* in to remove endangered barges from beside the docks.[5]

The shifting wind, now blowing from the north, increased to about thirty miles-per-hour, and pushed the fire south into the financial district and toward the piers adjacent to Pratt Street. Roaring through the financial district, the fire consumed many of Baltimore's investment and insurance companies and banks. Flames engulfed the Chamber of Commerce building, the Stock Exchange, and the Merchant's Club. The corner of Calvert and Baltimore Streets, where the skyscrapers of the Baltimore & Ohio Railroad and Continental Trust Company stood, became a hellish maelstrom, with tempera-

tures reaching 2,500 degrees. Wooden paving blocks and asphalt burned in the roadbeds, and the resin in wooden timbers exploded.[6] As the fire tore through the financial district, it seemed to consume everything in its path,

The fire at 3:00 A.M. Monday, as it looked from Federal Hill, across the basin. MdHS.

Night Scene, Baltimore's Great Fire, February 1904.

A color postcard representing a scene at night, in the heart of the fire. MdHS.

but for a few astonishing exceptions. The only damage to the red stone, Romanesque fortress housing the Safe Deposit and Trust Company included several broken windows and a burned desk in the president's office. It seems that painters had left some flammable material there and the heat from nearby burning buildings ignited it. Other than that, the fire spared the building. The Mercantile Trust and Deposit Company on the northwest corner of German and Calvert Streets, and the Alex. Brown and Sons building on the southwest corner of Baltimore and Calvert also survived. The rather squat Alex. Brown building probably survived because the updraft from

the surrounding buildings carried the flames up and over it, although the intense heat cracked some of its stonework.[7]

At 2:30 A.M. Monday, the fire expanded southwest and attempted to cross Charles Street below Lombard. Two volunteer fire companies—twenty-five young firefighters—put up a splendid defense. Using old-fashioned hand engines they pumped water vigorously to the cheers of hundreds of spectators, but their heroic efforts failed. By 3 A.M., the fire was spreading to the east side of Charles Street.

In the midst of all this danger, commotion, and excitement, evidence arose that surely confirms the belief that God protects drunks and fools. A stream of water intended for a building on Calvert Street mistakenly hit a well-dressed businessman walking along St. Paul Street, parallel to Calvert. He had been drinking heavily and weaved from side to side, wondering no doubt about the source of his sudden, discomforting dampness. Upon finally realizing that the water was coming from above, he looked up, lost his balance, and fell in a puddle. Two policemen helped him up, replaced his hat, and sent him home.[8]

Speaking with a *Sun* reporter at 3:30 A.M., McLane, apparently unaware of the fire spreading in the south, said, "I feel the conflagration shows some signs of abating." Police Marshal Farnan, when asked responded, "I think the fire is practically under control." By 4 A.M., however, the north side of Pratt Street stretching east almost to the Jones Falls stood ablaze. Burning turpentine and lumber emitted large clouds of smoke and left no doubt in anyone's mind that the fire would continue to grow. It destroyed the powerhouse of the United Railway & Electric Company, which collapsed about 4:30. Located on the south side of Pratt Street between Fredrick and Centre Market Space, the eleven engines in the powerhouse stopped generating electricity. Streetcars suddenly halted and streetlights went out. Outside the business district trolley service continued, however, as cars jammed with curious spectators tried to get a good look at the fire.[9]

The fire burning along the Charles Street corridor continued moving to the south, but by 5 A.M. it halted at Balderston Street, halfway between Lombard and Pratt Streets. Unfortunately, the fire one block to the west gained strength after setting warehouses containing chemicals and oils ablaze, then continued farther south to the Maltby

Hotel. The flames made quick work of the Maltby and moved on to Pratt Street. In the hours before dawn, firefighters found themselves forced back to the docks. They had to halt the fire north of the docks, on the south side of Pratt Street, or see the city's commercial hub—its aging wooden piers and wharves along the Pratt and Light Street edges of the harbor basin—destroyed. Here the freighters, coastal steamers, banana boats, and other commercial sailing ships all unloaded their cargoes.[10] After hasty coordination, much of it accomplished by shouting, firefighters moved all available engines in the southern portion

Surveying the damage on Lexington Street on Monday, after the fire has passed. Firemen examine a smoking upper story. MdHS.

of the fire zone into a line along the south side of Pratt Street.

In addition to those engines, the fireboat *Cataract* moved east and west along the waterfront, sending streams of water toward the fire at points where they could best have effect. The eighty-five-foot *Cataract*, built in 1891, was Baltimore's first fireboat. It had an eight-

een and a half foot beam and drew nine feet. With a pumping capability of 4,400 hundred gallons per minute, the *Cataract's* four guns shot streams of water on the burning structures and lumberyards near the waterfront. When not actively fighting the fire, she supplied water to land-based fire engines working closer to the flames.[11] The fire engines

Citizens behind a fire line at City Hall on East Fayette Street look south down Commerce Street. The time is uncertain, but might be early Monday afternoon, as the fire sweeps toward the docks. Umbrellas offered some protection against falling ash and cinders. MdHS

and the *Cataract* drew water from the basin and propelled it with considerable force, but the strong wind in the firemen's faces diffused the streams, dispersing the torrents and rendering many of them ineffective.

With the buildings along Pratt Street hopelessly ablaze and the financial district already in ruins, attention now turned to defending East Baltimore. This revised fire-fighting strategy, called by some "the last line of defense," had as its object preventing the fire from crossing the Jones Falls. The wind still blew hard from the northwest and north. Although firemen were still fighting mightily to save the docks, if they were lost the basin itself would stop the fire

there, but to the east lay highly combustible lumberyards, other flammable sites, Little Italy, and other residential areas. Firefighters grimly took up stations on the eastern shore of the Jones Falls, thirty-seven fire engines from Baltimore Street and the falls all the way south to the Block Street draw-bridge.

Elsewhere in Maryland the sky was clear that Monday morning, but on the fire lines the rising sun, barely visible through the hellish smoke, told exhausted men from Maryland, Pennsylvania, and Washington, D.C., that another harrowing day's work lay ahead. Property owners on the northern and western fringes of the fire might relax

By noon Monday the fight was on the waterfront. MdHS See also pages 94–95.

93

The view southeast from the Continental Trust Building. This is how Baltimore looked late on Monday. MdHS

Family and friends bring hot coffee to firefighters. MdHS

for the moment, though a shift in the wind could at any time swiftly change their fortunes. And many of the spectators who had flocked to see the most significant event in Baltimore since the Great Railroad Strike of 1877 had returned home long before dawn. The few who remained, hoping to see the fire cornered, and the firemen hoping it might be so, were wrong. Far from dying, the fire raged.

The spectacular destruction of the Maryland Institute and the Church of the Messiah shortly after midnight had made an impression on the inhabitants of Little Italy as they watched from the other side of the Jones Falls. Fearing their neighborhood would be next as the fire roared eastward in Monday's pre-dawn hours, some threw bedding and clothing out of windows and stacked furniture and possessions on the sidewalk in preparation for flight. As the sun rose, the crowd in Little Italy attempting to evacuate to the east swelled and the tempo increased. Teamsters who had gained experience gouging prices in the business district the day before soon appeared to line their pockets again.

Sidewalks jammed by household goods forced people into the street, where, arms filled with possessions, they had to dodge fast-moving wagons and horses. The street itself was soon crowded with people, handcarts, makeshift wagons, and teamsters trying to earn a quick profit. With tension mounting, some residents panicked, while others stood numbly in tears. Attendants on the harbor ferries at the foot of Broadway, who feared overloading their vessels, added to the trials of those trying desperately to evacuate by turning away many Little Italy residents from ferries that could have taken them to safety in Locust Point. Storeowners along Broadway began stacking their wares on the sidewalk in front of their shops and searching for transportation. Before long, the teamsters with wagons for hire found the Broadway merchants to be better clients than the residents

View from the Jones Falls at Baltimore Street looking southwest after the fire had been stopped. The four smokestacks of the power plant are barely visible through the haze. MdHS

of Little Italy. Feeling that salvation now could only come from above, parishioners packed into St. Leo's Church to pray to St. Anthony. And as they prayed, their thoughts focused on the Jones Falls and its role as the protective barrier that could stop the fire from spreading to their homes.

At this stage of the conflagration, the shifting wind moved the fire in many different directions, in some cases returning it to blocks already severely damaged and destroying buildings previously bypassed. Moving east along the north side of Pratt Street, the fire advanced as far as the Jones Falls, then jumped to the other side of Pratt Street and traveled

Pratt Street looking south down Dugan's Wharf, guarded by a member of the Naval Brigade. MdHS back moving west as far as Cheapside. Firefighters manning the thirty-seven engines in position along East Falls Road, parallel to the Jones Falls, shot streams of water across the waterway, using the unlimited water supply of the falls to soak everything within range. It looked for awhile like they would halt the fire. Some engine crews even set up on the many east-west bridges crossing this narrow waterway to get closer to the flames. One crew on the Lombard Street Bridge got closer to the fire than it expected but held its ground as the bridge itself caught fire, burned, and appeared ready to collapse, forc-ing them to withdraw. The heat from the fire on the opposite shore remained intense. For the moment, the Jones Falls which Baltimoreans referred to as a "miserable dirty stream" and a source of miasmic vapors, appeared to be the city's savior.[12]

As the morning progressed, flames engulfed the docks. At the same time, firefighters made little progress in stopping the fire from moving east. Those structures that still stood west of the Jones Falls fell one by one. South of Pratt Street, almost every building on the west side of the falls stood ablaze. The heat and embers from burning stacks of

In the first hours after the fire, spectators coming to view the tragedy first hand were shocked at the fire's destruction. Buildings were reduced to shells, and rubble filled the streets. Enoch Pratt Free Library

Looking north from the
harbor at the ruins of
Cheapside. From
*Photographic Views and
Description of the Great
Baltimore $175,000,000 Fire,
February 7–9, 1904*
(Baltimore: E. B. Read &
Son Co., 1904).

lumber west of the falls threatened to ignite stacks of lumber on the east side. Flames destroyed the T. J. Meyer Packing Company's warehouse and engulfed the building of the Boyer Fruit Packing Company, as well as the plant of the Maryland Ice Company. The fire also ignited lumberyards and packinghouses on the nearby Union Dock. The *Cataract,* firing streams of water, moved close to the burning Union Dock and had some success extinguishing flames on portions of it.

In addition to the *Oriole* and the intrepid fireboat *Cataract,* numerous other firefighting boats and ships joined the fight. Later on

Monday morning, the *Windom,* a revenue cutter, steamed from Annapolis, helped battle the fire on the docks, and aided B&O workers trying to rescue bags of coffee from a warehouse in the path of the blaze. The decks of *Windom* and another government steamer, *Potomac,* were soon piled with sacks of coffee. The *Neptune,* an unfinished tug towed away from the shore, took aboard material from a warehouse in the path of the fire, later returning the goods worth about $15,000.

Between 11 A.M. and 1 P.M., embers and firebrands propelled across the Jones Falls started several substantial fires, including one in the lumber stacked next to a building housing the Broadbent and Davis Mantel Company at President Street and Canton Avenue. Firemen managed to save the building and extinguished the fire on the roof of Otto Ducker's box factory. The most substantial fires arose near Thames and Philpot Streets, where fire destroyed Isaac Robinson's Fertilizer Works, the L. Sonneborn & Son Chemical Company, and the Maine Lake Ice Company. Then, in an all-out effort, the combined Washington and Baltimore fire companies stopped the flames from spreading further and destroying the volatile Shryock Lumber Yard on Philpot near Thames, containing about five million feet of lumber. Between 1:00 and 1:30, Francis Denmead's Malt House caught fire. New Yorkers rushed to contain it before its volatile supply of malt particles could threaten Canton. No sooner had they

put out the fires than the building reignited. This time they suppressed the fire for good.

Having finally brought the fires east of the falls under control, firefighters turned their attention back to the nearby Savanna pier off West Falls Avenue at Block Street. Occupied by the Merchants & Miners' Transportation Company, it had lumber stacked on it and had burst into flames three times that afternoon. Initially, an improvised fireboat consisting of a steam launch rigged with a huge wooden bucket sailed as close as it could to the flames, then maneuvered the bucket over the flames and dumped water on them. That was not enough, but soon the clever crews on the tugboats *Venus* and *Mary* joined their efforts with those of Baltimore and New York City firefighters and saved the Savannah pier. Having quelled the fire at Denmead's Malt House, a New York fire

LEFT AND RIGHT: The view from Federal Hill across the harbor to the remains of the fire. MdHS

company and Baltimore's No. 11 rushed to the pier, but it was at once obvious that their water streams could not reach the flames far out on the end. At that moment the *Venus* and the *Mary,* vessels belonging to businesses on the pier, steamed through the smoke. The fireboat *Cataract* joined in the fight, and all three delivered powerful streams of water onto the dock. A shift in the wind helped greatly. As it turned, now coming from the south, it blew flames back into areas already destroyed. Firefighters soon brought the fire at Savannah pier under control, ending the last threat to East Baltimore and bringing the Great Baltimore Fire to an end.

George W. Horton, struck by electric

wires around noon on Sunday, returned to duty at 1:30 Monday afternoon, relieving District Engineer Emrich and directing the final efforts to control the fire.[13] West of the falls, the business and financial district was naught but smoking rubble. The last structure to burn was, ironically, a large ice storage shed on West Falls Road. The American Ice Company building contained Kennebec ice insulated by wooden walls, sawdust preservative, and sawdust between layers of ice. Although fire destroyed the building, an immense cone of ice incongruously remained in the center of the smoking ruins. With the destruction of the ice shed, the worst was past, but the ghastly shells of buildings and

A view across the harbor from the base of Federal Hill right after the fire. Much of the area still smolders. MdHS

Destroyed buildings, now a
total loss to their owners
also presented a danger—
and additional costs to tear
down their weakened walls
and remove the rubble.
Enoch Pratt Free Library.

piles of rubble continued to smolder, re-ignit-
ing here and there long after officials deemed
the fire officially out.

Because no one seemed to remember
precisely when the flames died down or
exactly when the firefighters extinguished the
blaze in the icehouse, a range of statements
proclaim varying times when the Baltimore
Fire actually ended. In its official report, the
Baltimore fire department said that the "conflagration raged until 11:30 A.M. Monday,"
perhaps referring to when the fire seemed to
lose its force. The *Baltimore Herald* claimed,
"The Great Fire was out between 2 and 3
o'clock." The *Sun* reported "the fire was officially declared under control at 5 P.M." The
distance of the Savannah pier and the icehouse from City Hall and downtown
Baltimore could explain the varied opinions
about when firefighters brought the fire under
control.

The efforts of many had conquered the
Great Baltimore Fire, but the results were
devastating. The entire area that Baltimore's
city founders had laid out in 1729 was now a
bleak landscape of hollowed buildings, smoking ash, and rubble.[14] Apparently no one had
died. Authorities could not substantiate the
rumor that a man on fire had run off the end
of a burning dock and perished. With no
body or report of a missing person, and no
witnesses to the event, officials could not confirm it had happened.[15] Firefighters watched
over the numerous and persistent smaller fires
while soldiers attempted to isolate the burnt
district and kept an eye out for looters.
Throughout the city, citizens began taking
stock of all that had been lost.

The Great Fire is
Still Smoking

SPARKS FROM THE STORY OF BALTIMORE'S FIRE continue to smolder, and new embers probably are yet to be uncovered in century-old newspapers from Baltimore and throughout the nation. Although practically every account of the fire since 1904 reported that no one perished in the blaze, a discovery by an under-graduate at the Johns Hopkins University in 2003 challenges that claim.

Completing his bachelor's degree in history, James Collins conducted research in support of a senior thesis about the Baltimore fire, and while combing through countless 1904 newspaper articles he found "a tiny, three-inch story titled 'One Life Lost in Fire' while reading the February 17, 1904, issue of *The Sun*," according to a story in Baltimore's *City Paper*.[1] Collins learned that Navy guards-men on duty along the southern edge of the fire zone retrieved the charred remains of an African-American man from the "basin [now known as the inner harbor] at Bowley's Wharf," near the mooring of the *USS Sylvia*, home to the Naval Brigade Headquarters.[2]

Collins pursued the story and considered it "odd how everyone glossed over finding this body." He found that even the city's *Afro-American* newspaper failed to report it. Searching further, Collins found "a death certificate dated February 24, 1904, for an unidentified burned and waterlogged black man whose unclaimed remains were ultimately cremated."[3]

Although no one ever was reported missing during or after the fire, Collins speculates that the deceased man may have been a hero who gave his life while helping to remove goods stacked on the wharf. The flames could have trapped him as they raged south that fateful night and the next day. It also is possible that he may have been one of several vagrants who had been on the wharves as the fire approached.

Searching for a reason why this possible casualty of the fire was never reported, Collins considers that Baltimore's civic pride may have deterred changing zero fatalities to one fatality. "Another (and uglier) reason might have to do with racism," noted the *City Paper*. Officials may not have deemed a single black life sufficient in 1904 to warrant undercutting the supposed—and astounding—lack of deaths related to the fire.

Just as the mystery of the dead man's identity may never be determined, so the cause behind his demise and the reasons it went unreported may remain forever mysterious—just as is the exact cause of how the fire got started.

---

[1] Brennen Jensen, "Lives Lost: One," *The City Paper*, September 13, 2003, p. 18

[2] "One Life Lost in Fire," *The Sun*, February 20, 1904.

[3] *City Paper*, Sept. 3, 2003, p. 18.

HEART OF BALTIMORE WRECKED BY GREATEST FIRE IN CITY'S HISTORY

A THOUSAND BUILDINGS BURNED; LOSS OVER $75,000,000

DYNAMITE USED TO COMBAT FLAMES IN VAIN—ALL OF CHIEF SKYSCRAPERS DESTROYED

EXTRA ENGINES BROUGHT HERE FROM ALL THE NEIGHBORING CITIES

ENTIRE DISTRICT BETWEEN HOWARD AND GAY, FAYETTE AND PRATT STREETS IN RUINS

ON HOPKINS PLACE.

ALONG LOMBARD STREET.

Explosion Followed Explosion.

Big Buildings Dynamited.

Engines From Other Cities.

Block After Block Burned.

Leaped Across Baltimore Street.

Dragging Books to Safety.

Martial Law Declared.

Skyscrapers Fall.

Newspapers Burned Out.

REGULARS ON DUTY.

Men From Fort McHenry Guard Government Buildings.

Council Meets This Morning.

MILITIA CALLED OUT.

They Were Ordered to Assemble to Protect Property.

CITY HOSPITAL THREATENED.

Appeals for Beds Were Promptly Met by Neighboring Institutions.

JACKSON BUILDING ESCAPED.

With Flames All About It, It Did Not Burn.

FIFTY OUT

ZION CHURCH

THE HERALD

⇒ 5 ⇐

Four Baltimore Dailies Burned Out

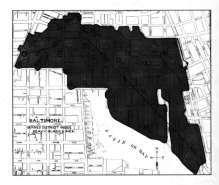

"HOT OFF THE PRESS" quickly became more than a cliché that Sunday morning, as the fire spread with alarming speed. Reporters for the city's five daily newspapers dashed to their offices and began working on the biggest story since the Civil War. Before the blaze died out, the presses in four of those five publications would know the heat of the flames.

February had begun as a slow news month, H. L. Mencken recalled nearly forty years later, but that was about to change. The reporter who rushed to Mencken's house at 1524 Hollins Street shortly after the smoke explosion in the Hurst building was quite correct in telling him, "The fire looked to be a humdinger, and promised swell pickings for a dull winter Sunday."[1] As the conflagration raged, reporters from other cities arrived in Baltimore and joined in the news frenzy. Their dispatches by telephone and telegraph formed the city's strongest link with the outside world. City-dwellers up and down the Eastern Seaboard and into the Midwest read the latest dispatches about the disaster on bulletin boards outside newspaper offices.

News of the fire raging in a sister city was compelling. Hometown reporters interviewed passengers as they arrived on trains from Baltimore. As might be expected, some travelers exaggerated. Others related rumors rather than fact. Initial reports during catastrophes are often wrong, and those describing the fire in Baltimore were no exception. The *Harrisburg Telegraph* inaccurately reported that a falling structure had killed a firefighter from nearby York at Baltimore and Frederick Streets. On February 9 the *New York Times* reported, "Only two lives were lost. One was a fireman from York, and the news spread about Baltimore to the effect that a New York fireman had lost his life."[2] The *Times* story appeared the day after firefighters had brought the fire under control but had doubtless been filed while the situation was still chaotic. With a little more time, New York reporters on the scene would have known that these reports were false.

Although the fire disrupted some telephone and telegraph services, Baltimore had alternate means for contacting other cities. In fact, at all times during the fire, some form of telephone communication was working in Baltimore outside the fire zone. Even within the threatened area, telephone service continued in the Central Telephone Exchange Building on St. Paul Street until supervisors told operators to leave their switchboards around 9:20 P.M. on Sunday.3 Maintaining telegraph service involved different challenges. On Sunday evening, the fire cut off Baltimore's two central telegraph offices from the rest of the country. The *New York Times* reported that, "After 9 o'clock last night no messages of any kind were received from the stricken city through the central offices. The men who were at the keys in the office worked fast until the flames came too close."4 In one case, the Western Union operator at the *Philadelphia Inquirer* received only part of a dispatch. The Baltimore operator then tapped out, "Good-bye old man. We are ordered out by the fire chief," before fleeing the fire.5

As the fire expanded, it burned out four Baltimore dailies, including the *Herald*, with its precocious city editor, twenty-three-year-old Mencken. The homeless papers moved thirty-five miles to Washington, D.C., and kept the presses rolling. In almost six weeks following the fire, the staff of the *Herald* moved four times and published their paper from three places. The *Baltimore Sun* made arrangements with the *Washington Evening Star* to use its composing room, and, after the *Star* put its paper to bed, to use its presses as well. That operation continued until April 6. The *Baltimore American* resumed publication Tuesday, February 9, from the building of Frank A. Munsey's *Washington Times* and stayed there until February 27. A fourth paper, the *Baltimore Evening News,* had a long-standing agreement with the

The Baltimore Herald Building before the fire. Published by permission of the Enoch Pratt Free Library in accordance with the terms of the bequest of H. L. Mencken.

The Herald Building after the fire. From *The Brickbuilder,* 1904. Courtesy Enoch Pratt Free Library.

Washington Post to share its facilities in the event of a calamity. Luckily, the fire did not affect a fifth paper, the *Baltimore World.*

But the real action was at the *Herald.* Mencken had a grand view of the expanding fire from the fifth-floor editorial offices. Like other occupants of "fireproof" buildings, he thought his was safe. That false sense of security combined with what can only be described as bravado led reporters and editors to stay in the *Herald* building, watching the flames close in around them. Because they did not expect to leave the building, much less be burned out, many thought they shortly would be returning to their desks when officials evacuated the *Herald* around 9 P.M. Sunday so that a demolition crew could blow up a building across the street. Two key members of the staff—Joe Bamberger, foreman of the composing room, and Joe Callahan, Mencken's assistant—were less optimistic.

Bamberger carried out page-proofs, galley proofs, and copy not yet set. He also had the foresight to save the front-page logotype of the *Herald* and about a dozen half-tones. Callahan scooped up copy left behind in the city room, Associated Press items about the opening of the Russo-Japanese war, and a few office supplies. After the move, Mencken wrote little copy but instead ran the shop and accomplished what one would expect from a first-rate city editor. He wrote the headline for Monday morning's paper, "Heart of Baltimore Wrecked by Greatest Fire in City's History"—on a make-up table in the

Washington Post's composing room, while *Herald* managing editor Lynn Meekins wrote a box for the front page thanking the *Post* for its "proverbial courtesy to its contemporaries."[6]

Meekins wasted no time once his offices were lost. As the *Herald* building was going up in flames, he contacted Scott C. Bone, managing editor of the *Washington Post,* who agreed to help but explained that assistance would be limited because the long-standing agreement between the *Post* and the *Baltimore Evening News* was about to push the *Post* to its limits.

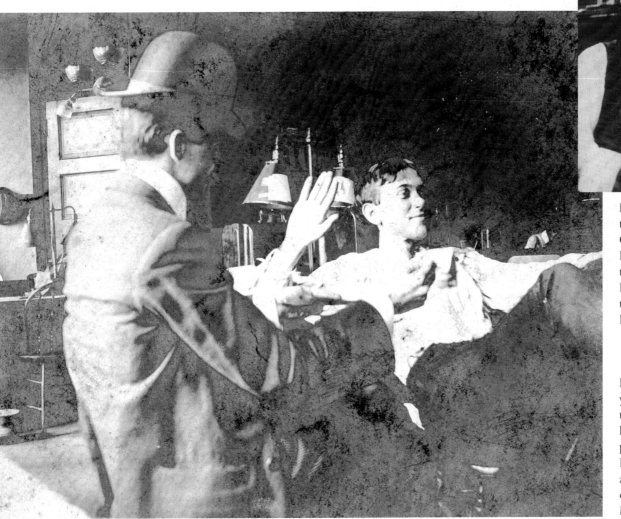

H. L. Mencken in his new, temporary office on South Charles Street after the fire. Published by permission of the Enoch Pratt Free Library in accordance with the terms of the bequest of H. L. Mencken.

H. L. Mencken, the cocky young newspaperman, in the *Herald* offices early in his career. Published by permission of the Enoch Pratt Free Library in accordance with the terms of the bequest of H. L. Mencken

Ruins of the Junker Hotel on the north side of Fayette between Charles and St. Paul Streets, a few doors west of the Herald building. H. L. Mencken had joined his friends at the Stevedore Club there past midnight Saturday, after putting the Sunday paper to bed. Courtesy Deutsche Bank Alex. Brown

Arriving in Washington around midnight, Meekins in a matter of hours produced a four-page *Herald* after the February 8 issue of the *Post* had gone to bed. Understanding that the *Post* could not accommodate both the *Evening News* and his paper, Meekins looked around and, discovering that the *Baltimore World* had not suffered from the fire, quickly reached an agreement permitting the *Herald* to return to Baltimore and publish from its competitor's facilities. A small afternoon paper, the *World* could produce its daily edition after the presses had spent the night printing the morning *Herald*. This convenient arrangement lasted all of a day. The *World's*

Linotype machines broke down, and the amount of type that could be set by hand proved inadequate. Learning that the *Catholic Mirror*, a Baltimore weekly, might have adequate type, Meekins arranged to use some of their type at the *World,* but as luck would have it the *Mirror's* type proved to be of faulty quality and lacked adequate numbers of a uniform size.

Again, Meekins cast about for answers. Since the available facilities in Baltimore and Washington were insufficient, he considered moving operations to another city. Wilmington, Delaware, about seventy miles to the north, had only small papers with plants

Although the Herald building was in ruins, this wooden building beside it on St. Paul Street was unharmed, perhaps because it had no windows to admit firebrands. MdHS.

inadequate for the *Herald*. Although it was home to several large newspapers, Philadelphia was even farther away, one hundred miles from Baltimore. Meekins considered relocation to Philadelphia feasible if adequate transportation could be found, so he checked with Oscar G. Murray, president of the Baltimore and Ohio Railroad. Murray, now in his temporary office at a storage warehouse at Camden Station, was not without problems himself. The B&O headquarters building in Baltimore had been destroyed. He nevertheless agreed that at 2 A.M. each morning a train consisting of a locomotive, baggage car, and coach would stand by in Philadelphia with orders to dash to Baltimore loaded with

copies of the *Herald* printed in the City of Brotherly Love. Having found his transportation, Meekins reached an agreement with the *Philadelphia Evening Telegraph,* and there the *Herald* lived for the next five weeks.

Edwin F. Abell, president of the A. S. Abell Company, publishers of the *Sun*, was gravely ill, but his son, Walter, managed the paper in his absence after a fashion that would have made the father proud.[7] Beginning early Sunday afternoon, not long after the fire started, Abell and Edward Crummer, the *Sun's* business manager, assembled ledgers, other financial documents, and subscriber lists for safekeeping away from their threatened building. "The moving . . . began at 4 PM, and was hastened by the nearer and nearer approach of the flames," noted a 1905 company publication. Workers moved much of the material to the *Sun's* job-printing building at the southwest corner of Calvert and Saratoga Streets. Here workers collected news of the fire and later forwarded it by telegraph or messenger

The Herald building was protected by metal shutters, one of several safeguards that led employees to believe it truly was fireproof. Once the fire got inside the building it blew the shutters outward. MdHS

Mencken and the *Herald* staff put this edition of the paper together in the offices of the *Washington Post*. Mencken wrote the headline in the *Post's* composing room. Published by permission of the Enoch Pratt Free Library in accordance with the terms of the bequest of H. L. Mencken.

to the paper's relocated staff in Washington.[8]

Well before the fire threatened, Abell had prudently telegraphed the *Washington Star,* asking to use its facilities in the event his paper had to evacuate the famed Sun Iron Building on the southeast corner of Baltimore and South Streets. Remaining in the Iron Building, renowned for its ornamental iron façade, the *Sun's* staff were working on Monday morning's paper even as their compatriots across the street at the *American* streamed out of their building at 6 P.M. "It was a swell day for young journalists, and they enjoyed it immensely. Their city editor, Herbert A. Hallett, was a hard driver, but he did not have to urge them now," a history of the *Sun* later recalled. As the fire advanced toward their building *Sun* employees acting as

fireguards stood outside and at upper-story windows, ready to alert everyone if the building caught fire. Shortly before 10 P.M., as they were finishing Monday morning's edition, a printer saw a shower of sparks on the composing room skylight. He ran to Walter Abell and convinced him to evacuate. When Abell ordered everyone out of the building, much of the staff, thinking the printer had overreacted, resisted leaving and attempted to convince Abell to change his mind. Hallett insisted that in fifteen more minutes they could get the paper printed, but Abell stood firm. "We'll take no chances with men's lives. . . . I'd never forgive myself if a single man should lose his life, or get seriously hurt," he said.[9] As his staff departed, Abell dashed back inside to be sure the building stood empty.

EXTRA! BALTIMORE MORNING HERALD

ESTABLISHED 1875—WHOLE NUMBER 9073   MONDAY, FEBRUARY 8, 1904.

HEART OF BALTIMORE WRECKED BY GREATEST FIRE IN CITY'S HISTOR

A THOUSAND BUILDINGS BURNED; LOSS OVER $75,000,0

DYNAMITE USED TO COMBAT FLAMES IN VAIN—ALL OF CHIEF SKYSCRAPERS DESTRO

EXTRA ENGINES BROUGHT HERE FROM ALL THE NEIGHBORING

ENTIRE DISTRICT BETWEEN HOWARD AND GAY, FAYETTE AND PRATT STREETS IN

Told to convene at the Lexington Hotel opposite City Hall on Holliday Street, the *Sun* staff gathered and planned how to get to Washington to finish writing and printing the paper in the few hours they would have after the *Washington Star* finished its press run. Harold West went to the B&O headquarters at Calvert and Baltimore Streets to arrange for a special train to take them to Washington. The B&O Building itself had caught fire. Its roof was ablaze and sparks showered down the elevator, but the telegraph line there still worked. Arthur Hale, General Superintendent of Transportation, contacted the stationmaster at Camden Station, directing him to put together a train with two coaches behind the

fastest locomotive in the yards and clear a track to Washington. Fifteen minutes after this final bit of business concluded, the B&O building erupted completely.

At 11 P.M., as the *Sun*'s staff left the Lexington Hotel and headed toward Camden Station, reporter Frank R. Kent was sitting at the hotel bar writing the lead story for the Monday morning edition. He just managed to catch up with his colleagues as the train left for Washington. During the forty-five minute ride to the capital, Allen S. Will, the telegraph editor, assigned jobs to those who would produce the paper. Around midnight, the *American*'s building succumbed to the fire, and shortly thereafter the Sun Iron Building stood in flames.

The Sun Building, the first cast-iron structure in Baltimore. It was five stories high and had stood for fifty-four years. MdHS

After the *Sun* staff settled in at the *Evening Star,* one problem seemed unsolvable: the *Sun*'s page was larger than its host's. As a result, "the page matrixes prepared in Baltimore would not fit the *Star*'s casting box." Finally, someone found an unused casting box over at the *Washington Post,* and the *Sun* was in business.[10]

After a wild day and a fast-moving night, Baltimore newsboys sold two newspapers that had been printed in Washington and rushed north to the city early Monday morning, the second day of the fire. The *Sun* appeared in downtown Baltimore before 5 A.M., while twenty thousand copies of the *Herald*—transported in a baggage car—arrived in Baltimore by 8:45 A.M. Although the *Sun* and *Herald* normally sold for a penny, entrepreneurial hawkers peddled some of their papers for as much as a quarter to news-hungry readers.

The experiences of the *Baltimore Evening News* and the *Baltimore American* were no less memorable. At the *Evening News,* one comment from a legendary character became part of the company's lore. Dr. Frederick Taylor,

MORE MORNING HERALD

TUESDAY, FEBRUARY 9, 1904.   PRICE ONE CENT.

GREAT FIRE CONQUERED AT LAST; LEGISLATURE COMES TO CITY'S AID

ASSEMBLY DECLARES LEGAL HOLIDAYS TO PROTECT BUSINESS

President Roosevelt Sends U. S. Troops Under General Corbin to Baltimore to Preserve Order.

INSURANCE MEN NOW ESTIMATE THE LOSS AT FROM $100,000,000 TO $150,000,000

The great fire is over. At 2 o'clock yesterday afternoon it was under control and at 4 o'clock the final blaze was sputtering along the stringpiece of Union dock.

Of course, there are still scores of minor fires here and there among the ruins, but the "big fire" itself is out. Time and the ingenuity of men have conquered it, but in its raging it wrecked the entire business center of Baltimore, from Howard street to beyond the falls and from Fayette street to the water front. A hundred million dollars or more was its cost to the city. Now it is over and the work of reconstruction has begun.

A local insurance man said last

taining order and will relieve the tired militiamen. They were sent by President Roosevelt in response to a request from Governor Warfield.

The Legislature last night, in special session, passed, under a suspension of the rules, an act declaring yesterday, today, tomorrow, Thursday, Friday, Saturday, Sunday and Monday legal holidays, and authorizing the Governor to declare other holidays as he may deem necessary. The object of this legislation is to protect commercial interests. On the holidays declared all of the banks will remain closed.

The city council declared a ten-day legal holiday.

HELP FROM CHICAGO.

western progress of the fire and sent the flames biting viciously through the district lying west of the falls and south of Baltimore street. When dawn came the hottest part of the conflagration was all south of Canton avenue.

BATTLE FOR EAST BANK.

The fight then was to save the east side, as it was evident that once across the falls all hope of stemming the fiery tide would have to be abandoned. With this object in view all the engines which could possibly be spared from the other edges of the devastated area were stationed down the main battle line, which practically coincided with the course of Jones falls.

Each bridge across the falls was made a point of vantage to fight the flames. The Lombard street

up until 3 o'clock occurred at the intersection of Philpot and Thames streets.

Here the fertilizer works of Isaac Robinson & Co. and the L. Sonneborn & Son Chemical Company caught from sparks from the burning section of Union dock, and it looked for a time as if the brave fight to save the east side had been in vain. Two fire companies from Washington and Nos. 11, 15 and 18, from Baltimore, were hurried down President street and managed to extinguish the blaze after the Robinson Fertilizer and the Sonneborn Chemical companies had been gutted.

The part of Shryock's lumber yard facing the water was partially burned out, but the big barn, containing over 5,000,000 feet of lumber, was saved. If this had gone the Canton side would unquestionably

Herald, the American, the Sun, the Evening News, the Calvert building, the Law building, the Maryland Trust building, the Union Trust building, Putts' toy store, Hall, Headington & Co., Johnson, Boyd & Co., J. S. MacDonald & Co., the Consolidated Gas Co.

Oehm's Acme Hall, the Singer Sewing Machine Company, Imwold & Co., the Carrollton Hotel, the Southern Hotel, Armstrong, Cator & Co., R. Lertz & Co., Wm. T. Dixon & Bros., the Central Savings Bank, Pattison & Gahan, Junker's Hotel, the Fayette, the Daily Record building, the Glenn building, the McKim building, the Knabe building, the Hurst building, J. Seth Hopkins & Co., the Dulany building, the Goodyear Rubber Company, Henegan, Bates & Co., the International Trust Co., the Arminger Jewelry Company, the Hub, Thomas & Thompson, the Adams Express Company, the New York Clothing House, Samuel Kirk & Sons, the Ross drug store, the Baltimore and Ohio Central building, Alex Brown & Sons, the Telegram building, the Odeon Theater, the Fisher building, the Mer-the society editor, proclaimed as he fled the burning building just before 9 P.M. on Sunday night: "Thank God the roaches and water bugs are now dead!"[11] He then watched the building at Baltimore and Grant Streets go up in flames, apparently delighted that even if the building burned to the ground employees would at least have sweet revenge on those vermin. Taylor's remark remained a part of Baltimore folklore long after he was gone and the *Evening News* had folded.

The *American* and the *Evening News* had an agreement prior to the fire to help one another in the event of an emergency. When the fire destroyed both their buildings, they were left without a plan for coping with the emergency. The *American* began operating from the *Washington Times* building, while the offices of the *Washington Post* accommodated the printing of the *Evening News*. Although *Evening News* editor Charles H. Grasty started printing his paper at the *Post,* he also hoped that his friend, Adolph Ochs, publisher of the *New York Times*, could help him. Ochs had bought the *Philadelphia Times*, and having merged it with another paper had the *Philadelphia Times's* idle equipment on his hands. Forced to move quickly, Grasty "jumped on the midnight train and arrived early . . . [Monday] morning" in New York, in the hope of buying the vitally needed equipment. Telephoning Ochs at home, Grasty informed him "everything has been destroyed in Baltimore" and asked, "How about that *Philadelphia Times* plant?"

"That plant is at your service," Ochs replied.

"What's the price?" Grasty wanted to know.

"Go and take it, and if you and I can't agree upon the price later, why we'll leave the matter to a third party,"[12] said Ochs.

Grasty moved the essential equipment from Philadelphia to Baltimore by train within ten days and found a home for the machinery in an abandoned, dirt-floored foundry at Holliday and Centre Streets. After laying a wooden floor and interior walls, Grasty looked about for a means of providing the steam needed for power and heat. Since putting in a boiler would have taken too long, he bought an old locomotive, put it behind the foundry, took off its wheels, and soon had steam to power his presses.[13] The *News*, as well as the *American*, printed their papers at the *Washington Times* until Grasty's rapidly assembled plant in Baltimore opened, enabling both papers to use this improvised facility by the end of February.

After returning to Baltimore on April 6, the *Sun* operated with hastily obtained and assembled equipment, some of it original machinery from the paper that workers had managed to repair. They were most fortunate in being able to expand and use their still-existing facility, the job-printing office. This building, constructed in 1900, sat conveniently just two blocks north of the Burnt District. The *Herald*'s staff did not have the *Sun*'s good fortune obtaining accommodations when they returned to Baltimore, and found room only in an abandoned street-railway powerhouse on South Charles Street.[14] Located on Calvert Street, the *World* escaped the fire, but this small evening paper drew little attention.

After the fire, the competition for advertising focused on the *Sun* and its three rivals: the *News*, *American*, and *Herald*. Of these, the *Sun* considered the *News* to be its greatest rival, and with good reason. Not for many years would the other papers falter in competition, leaving the *Sun* as Baltimore's dominant newspaper.[15]

6

Recrimination, Rebuttal, and Regeneration

THE SMOKE HAD BARELY cleared when blame for the Great Fire began to spread as rapidly as had its flames. There seemed to be no reason for a fire to have raged out of control for thirty hours, leaving much of downtown Baltimore in ashes and rubble. Critics contended it should not have gotten out of control at all. Could something have been wrong with Baltimore's fire department? Less than six weeks prior to the great fire, George W. Gail Jr., president of the Fire Commission, had stated in his annual report to the mayor and city council that the fire department's equipment was "in the best possible condition, representing all that is best in modern fire-fighting machinery." Gail had also boasted that Baltimore's firefighting abilities compared "favorably with that of any other department in the country."[1]

If true, then perhaps the fault lay with the owners of buildings and how they protected them against potential fires. Chief Horton placed the blame of the great fire squarely on the John E. Hurst Company. Horton claimed that had there been a watch-

man at the Hurst building, any record of Baltimore's fires for February 7, 1904, would instead have read: "A slight fire in the basement of J. E. Hurst's building among packing cases, extinguished by the watchman." Other owners of buildings did not escape Horton's wrath as he focused on the proper construction of buildings. "The rapid spread of the fire at the early stage was principally on account of wood exposures and windows giving away, caused by heat and concussion," Horton contended.[2] Horton's claim of faulty construction had some support. "Had the Hurst building been provided with wire glass and metal frames it would have prevented the conflagration," reported William W. Emmert, a member of a Baltimore architectural firm.[3]

But New York Battalion Chief John P. Howe, who had commanded the Gotham firefighters sent to Baltimore, had some sharp criticisms of Baltimore's fire department. Interviewed in Baltimore on Monday night, a few hours after his New Yorkers had helped bring the fire under control, Howe turned to a *New York Times* reporter and leveled two major criticisms at the stricken city. First, he

FACING PAGE:
The streets have been partially cleared in this photograph, but the ruined shellls of many buildings remain standing in the fire's aftermath.
Enoch Pratt Free Library

thought it preposterous that Baltimore should have but twenty-five fire engine companies—the companies sent from New York numbered more than a third of Baltimore's total fire-fighting strength. Second, he believed Baltimore lacked a replacement plan for injured or ill firefighters. Having said that, Howe also praised Baltimore's firefighters as "a fine lot. We are glad to have been of aid." Howe also expressed his appreciation for the way the citizens of Baltimore had praised his New Yorkers.

Nevertheless, criticism of Baltimore's firefighters resumed when their comrades from out-of-town returned home and responded to local reporters' questions about their experience in Baltimore. Understandably, those who had come to Baltimore took great pride in how they had contributed to quelling the flames, but they

were not particularly kind to Baltimore's fire department when comparing it with their own. Disparaging comments quickly appeared in the *Philadelphia Inquirer*. The Philadelphians' pride appeared in the *Inquirer's* claim that "Philadelphians outside the fire department who witnessed the fire declare that the Philadelphia firemen worked like fiends, facing the seething cauldron of flame and daring to go to places that everyone else thought inaccessible." Only a day after firefighters brought the fire under control—indeed, as isolated structures in Baltimore still were burning—Philadelphia firemen returning from Baltimore disparaged Baltimore's equipment and ability to fight fires. One headline expressed a sort of consensus among those interviewed: "[Philadelphia firemen] Declare That Baltimore Firemen are Handicapped by Bad Equipment." The Philadelphians claimed

Panoramic view of the Burnt District taken after the fire from a site on Federal Hill, across the Baltimore harbor basin. MdHS

that Baltimore's department seemed "imperfectly equipped. Their hose is smaller than ours, and their attachments [are] not of the most modern type." (Firefighters from Washington said much the same thing, complaining that Baltimore's hydrants were suitable for only a smaller diameter fire hose.) Fireman William Young complained, "I saw but one ladder and saw no water towers the entire time I was in Baltimore." Although those Philadelphians interviewed generally discussed equipment failures, some sharply criticized Baltimore's strategy for fighting fires.[4]

The Philadelphians contended that firemen must fight a fire from the front; that is, to prevent it from spreading rather than trying to extinguish where it had been. "Members of the Baltimore companies did not display very good judgment in the way they went about subduing the flames, or else lacked the nerve to fight the fire from the front," reported the *Inquirer*. "The Baltimore firemen acted like a lot of schoolboys," claimed foreman Van Sciver. "Our method was so different from the Baltimore way that it almost surprised them. They would stand in the middle of the street and aim the streams of water at the windows but they did not go right at the fire as our men do." Richard D. Great, an operator at Philadelphia Fire Headquarters at Juniper and Race Streets, who saw the fire from inside the lines in Baltimore, also commented, "Our men got in front of the flames which is the Philadelphia way of fighting fires." Police Captain McCoach, who led the 150 Philadelphia patrolmen, telegraphed the public safety director on Monday, criticizing Baltimore's strategy of fighting the fire "from the side and rear,"

Copyright 1904

Looking west on
Baltimore Street from a
spot near the Jones Falls.
MdHS

whereas the Philadelphians fought it "from the front to head off the spread of flames." Another official agreed. "I am confident that such a fire could never occur in Philadelphia."[5]

Travelers who had gone through Baltimore during the blaze and arrived later in Philadelphia also criticized Baltimore's efforts. Interviewed on February 8 by the *Inquirer,* Edward F. Birch from Washington reported, "I have watched the methods of firefighters in many other cities and a mistake in my estimation was the effort to save buildings already blazing instead of trying to prevent other places from catching [fire]." Birch also reported, "Dynamiting buildings seemed to do no good at all — in fact, it only served to spread the flames by scattering huge clouds

SATURDAY GLOBE.

PRICE
FIVE
CENTS,

VOL. XXIII. UTICA, SATURDAY, FEBRUARY 13, 1904. NO. 39.

THE BURNING OF BALTIMORE, FEBRUARY 7-8, 1904.
One Hundred and Twenty-five Million Dollar Fire in Maryland's Metropolis; Exceeded Only by the Chicago Fire of 1871.

[Drawn for the Utica Saturday Globe from description and from a view taken from the Harbor.]

COURAGEOUS IN HER AFFLICTION.

BALTIMORE FACES THE FUTURE WITH DAUNTLESS SPIRIT.

The Sea of Flame Which Destroyed the Commercial Heart of the City and Entailed a Loss of $125,-000,000 Has Not Crushed Her.

THE "FIRE AREA" IN BALTIMORE.
GENERAL VIEW OF THE BURNED COMMERCIAL DISTRICT.

SECTIONAL VIEW OF THE BALTIMORE RUINS.

[Ruins at the corner of Pratt street avenue and Water street, showing the remains of the building of the Maryland Fire Insurance Company.]

JAPAN'S WARSHIPS SWEEP THE ORIENTAL SEAS!

MARVELOUS NAVAL VICTORIES OF THE ISLAND EMPIRE GIVE THE RUSSIAN BEAR A RUDE SHOCK.

Daring Japs Have Disabled Many of the Russian Vessels and Have Gained a Distinct Advantage—Cause of the War.

DISABLED BY JAPANESE TORPEDOES.

[CONTINUED ON FOURTH PAGE.]

The Utica *Saturday Globe* carried a photograph of Baltimore prior to the fire, looking north toward City Hall, and comprising the northeast portion of the fire zone. MdHS

of red hot embers and blazing fragments." L. H. Crosby, the New York salesman passing through Philadelphia, offered a different and more damning criticism. "If the Baltimore force had worked as hard when the fire first broke out as they did an hour afterward I do not think the destruction would have been so great." Crosby had been at the Hurst building during the early stages of the fire and it seemed to him that it took more than half an hour to throw the first stream of water on the building.[6]

Art Summerfield's comments to the *New York Times* were equally disparaging. Summerfield, who had been near the Hurst building when the fire started, claimed, "The Baltimore Fire Department has been going to decay for the last two years and was in a

THE "FIRE AREA" IN BALTIMORE.
CENERAL VIEW OF THE BURNED COMMERCIAL DISTRICT.

122

worse condition when this fire started than it ever was before."7 Summerfield did not limit his criticism to Baltimore's firefighters; he found fault as well with the fire departments from other cities that had come to help. "The engines from Philadelphia also made a poor showing, as did the little engines from Wilmington and York, Penn."8 However, he abundantly praised the New Yorkers and credited them with saving Baltimore from further destruction.

In contrast, the *Washington Post* was most generous in appraising Baltimore's fire-fighting efforts. Possibly its opinion was influenced

A ship, probably a bay steamer, returns to its dock in the basin beside the burned out hulks of buildings in what was once a thriving port.
Enoch Pratt Free Library

by the fact that it shared its facility for two weeks with the reporters and staff of the burned-out *Baltimore Evening News.* Most of the *Post*'s reporting seemed positive if not overgenerous. Nevertheless, the *Post* did accurately report two stories that defied a positive spin. One, headlined "Firemen's Efforts Futile," dealt with how the fire had gotten out of control, and another related the limitations of dynamite in forming a barrier to prevent a fire from spreading.[9]

Although Baltimore had adequate water pressure and volume, misinformation about the effectiveness of Baltimore's water service

appeared frequently in out-of-town newspapers, probably put there by firefighters infuriated by Baltimore's odd-sized hydrants. Inadequate coupling forced some firefighters to draw their water from the city's sewers, the Jones Falls, and in a few cases, the harbor basin. The canard about Baltimore's insufficient water supply also may have originated in interviews given by travelers from the beleaguered city. One casual observer told the *Philadelphia Inquirer*, "From the little I saw of the fire I don't believe Baltimore had proper water protection." This led to a headline:

"Baltimore's Water Supply Inefficient." The headline failed to convey the same traveler's contradictory observation, buried in the story: "I saw one hose simply attached to a fire plug without the force of an engine behind it, and a splendid stream was thrown." A telegram from the B&O Railroad to the director of public safety in Philadelphia at midnight Sunday added to the gloom as it passed on similar false information. "The fresh water supply of Baltimore is exhausted and the engines [from Philadelphia] have begun to pump salt water." This would render

Baltimore residents and businessmen, like these gathered behind a police line at Baltimore and Liberty Streets, were not immediately permitted into the Burnt District to inspect the ruins in the wake of the fire. MdHS

Only civil and military authorities and those with signed passes could do so. MdHS

Philadelphia engines useless. Adding to the false rumor, the story appeared under the headline "Water Exhausted and City is Helpless."[10]

After the initial wave of critical opinion voiced in out-of-town newspapers, the world turned to other things, Baltimoreans settled down, passions waned, and reality set in. Less

than a week after the fire, the stories reported elsewhere began to reflect Baltimore's high opinion of its heroic fire department. It had been one hell of a fire, out of control and impossible to stop for thirty hours. Baltimore firefighters had been there from the beginning, and had good cause for appearing less than aggressive to companies newly arrived—

by that time the men were exhausted. Criticism of Baltimore's fire hydrants was also unwarranted, for at the time American cities had more than six hundred different sizes and variations of fire hose couplings. No wonder many of the out-of-town hose couplings would not connect with hydrants. Lack of standardization was a national problem, not a local issue. When these facts became evident, there was no doubt that Baltimore could be proud of its firefighters, yet Baltimore also recognized that effectively fighting future fires would require some modernization of their equipment.

Numerous fortunes were seriously dented during the Great Fire, and gloom shrouded the homes of civic and business leaders. Not long after the fire, however, grounds for hope

The John S. Gittings Company Bank, on the edge of the Burnt District at East Fayette Street and Guilford was the only building on the block to survive. It opened a soup kitchen "for sufferers of the 1904 fire," who have formed a line into the building. MdHS

reappeared when New York creditors expressed their confidence in the ability of Baltimore businesses to rise from the ashes and prosper. Actually, these same New York creditors had much to lose if Baltimore did not repair itself. The *New York Times* echoed this sense of optimism on the day after the fire, when it proclaimed that New York creditors who held sizable accounts from Baltimore dry goods jobbers were not concerned about being paid. Since Baltimore then was the largest dry goods center between New York and New Orleans, burned warehouses would have an immediate impact on the dry goods trade, but the damaged businesses were "all solid and conducted by good merchants [who] have fully protected themselves." As a result, New York mill agents and commission merchants felt "not at all anxious as to the obligations" from Baltimore

UNCLE SAM: "That's the spirit! Just roll up your sleeves and"——
BALTIMORE: "Yes, come back in a short time and we'll show you the model American city."

This editorial cartoon reflects the city's pride in rebuilding. Entitled, "A New Baltimore in Process of Construction," Baltimore informs Uncle Sam that it will soon be a model American city. *Baltimore News,* February 12, 1904.

BELOW: "He's the Cynosure of All Eyes." Characters representing Philadelphia, Boston, New York, and Chicago observe Baltimore hard at work. *Baltimore News,* February 24, 1904.

because businesses soon would be back on their feet. Upbeat news followed the next day when the *Times* reported: "Baltimore plans a greater city, many millions in safe deposit vaults found intact . . . banks are sound."[11] The story emphasized that citizens and bankers felt confident that the city could rebuild without outside aid.

Rising spirits seemed infectious. The skeptical *Philadelphia Inquirer* became more conciliatory as it noted, "Baltimore's future is clearing as she struggles to recover." In addition, the "work of rehabilitation is being carried forward with splendid courage and temporary business places are opening." Baltimore's woes were also Philadelphia's opportunities. The *Inquirer* observed that Philadelphia merchants could profit by "seizing the opportunity to secure a still larger

View east along Pratt Street, showing the fire's path. MdHS

share of the Southern trade" from burned-out Baltimore merchants.[12] Philadelphia contractors, too, would benefit from the inevitable building boom in Baltimore.

By Thursday, February 11, only three days after the fire, Baltimore's business leaders were displaying an aggressive approach to rebuilding. They had every reason to be optimistic. Encouraged by the New York banks' willingness to assist in financing and the readiness of most insurance companies to pay fire insurance claims, Baltimore's business leaders sensed the arrival of a construction boom. "Everyone will want to occupy the buildings first erected," reported the *New York Times*. With a backdrop of smoking ruins, Baltimore's leaders made plans for building new offices and stores. As might be expected, construction companies throughout the region solicited contracts. "We are going to recover fast," claimed President John R. Ramsey of the National Mechanics Bank adding, "The future presents no cause for anxiety." Ramsey also reported that his company "received $1,000,000 from New York today." James Bond, president of the American Bonding and Trust Company, had the good fortune that the fire did not harm his firm's vaults in the Equitable Building. Resuming business at Courtland and Saratoga Streets,

The ruins of the John E. Hurst building, where the fire originated. MdHS

Bond declared, "The next thing to do is rebuild," adding, "we'll do that as soon as possible." President John M. Littig of the National Marine Bank, whose building burned, set up his business temporarily on Calvert Street and joined his colleagues in declaring that he intended to construct another building.[13]

Many wondered what the future would bring for themselves and their city. The inhabitants of the half-mile square Italian enclave were overjoyed when firefighters defeated the flames at the edge of their neighborhood. Yet, while Little Italy's residents returned to their homes and danced in the streets, a group of German immigrants had a very different reaction. The North German Lloyd steamer *Willehad*, unable to dock as the fire raged on

Baltimore street sweepers—White Wings—dressed in white, began clearing the streets within days after the fire. MdHS

Monday, finally disembarked 470 passengers Tuesday. The sight of such devastation upon arriving in a new country shattered the confidence of some immigrants, who wanted to take the ship immediately back to Germany.

The Great Fire was for many a defining moment. For some it was a prelude to good fortune; for others, it beckoned tragedy. Three stories illustrate how the same event had profoundly different effects on three lives.

Robert M. McLane Jr.

Something of a political golden boy, Robert M. McLane was just thirty-five, when he became Baltimore's youngest mayor, elected on May 5, 1903.[14] Although his path to victory had not been smooth, he more than justified the faith of his supporters with effective leadership in fighting the massive fire just nine months later. Yet after the fire, McLane's talents and composure were stretched to the

A street sweeper, or "White Wing," clears coils of ruined fire hose. MdHS

The sign in the image reads:

IT'S ALL GONE, BUT, WITH HEALTH, FRIENDS
AND PROVIDENCE, WE'LL WIN AGAIN.
GIVE US ORDERS FOR ALL KINDS OF STONE,
OR SLATE WORK, MANTELS, TILING, MONUMENTS OR
HEADSTONES, AND WE WILL SUPPLY YOU AT MODERATE PRICES.
NOW OVER AT Nº 16   Wᵐ A. GAULT & SON,
E. LEXINGTON ST.   LATE 9 E. LEXINGTON ST.

breaking point, as he attempted to resolve the bickering among Baltimore's leading citizens, who battled endlessly over plans to reconstruct the business district. Perhaps his private life placed additional demands on him.[15] Married on May 14, 1904, just three months after the fire, it might be that he could not balance the weight of that commitment with the unceasing post-fire controversies with which he had to deal.

McLane was born in Baltimore on November 20, 1867, the son of James L. McLane, a wealthy businessman, and nephew of a former governor of Maryland, Robert M. McLane, who also had been minister to France during President Grover Cleveland's first administration. Young Robert showed exceptional abilities early on, entering the new Johns Hopkins University at just sixteen and completing the classical course in three

A lone trooper passes the former location of Wm. A. Gault & Son, a construction firm. Their sign combines a spirit of optimism and determination together with a more practical message. MdHS

Maryland National Guardsmen patrol Baltimore Street at Frederick. MdHS

years. Graduating at the age of nineteen, he remained at Hopkins for an additional year with a scholarship to pursue a graduate course in history. Near the end of 1888, McLane entered the University of Maryland School of Law, where he graduated at the head of his class. He then entered a private law practice with his brother Allan in 1891 before his appointment as one of the assistants

to Charles G. Kerr, the state's attorney of Baltimore. In 1895 he became deputy state's attorney to Henry Duffy, then left the office in 1897 to travel in Europe. Returning to Baltimore in 1899, McLane got himself elected state's attorney, and then in 1903 he won the Democratic Party nomination for mayor after a rigorous primary campaign against Mayor Thomas G. Hayes, Ferdinand C. Latrobe, and

Francis E. Yewell. The primary battle between McLane and Hayes was particularly intense, and with little let-up so was the general election, which McLane managed to win by a slim majority of 624 votes against Republican Frank C. Wachter. Wachter refused to concede and contested the bitter campaign for mayor in the Superior Court of Baltimore City.

Wachter challenged the results on grounds that election workers did not count ballots cast in four precincts, and further that they erroneously disallowed various ballots. McLane conceded that workers did not count the four precincts' ballots and, in his capacity as state's attorney, ordered them to be counted—thereby narrowing the gap between him-

self and Wachter to only 394 votes (47,290 for McLane to 46,896 for Wachter). The contested precincts also contained a number of defaced ballots, which the supervisor of elections had disallowed. In reversing an earlier decision not to count the defaced ballots, the court found that "the defacing marks were, in the opinion of the Court, either the result of careless handling by the elections officials or a deliberate attempt to disfranchise certain voters." Of the seventy-six defaced ballots the court reviewed, seventy-three had been cast for Wachter and three for McLane. Wachter then sought a recount in all precincts, but the court found that only 240 ballots had been rejected in all other precincts. Had Wachter won all 240 of

Baltimore's mounted police initially patrolled inside the fire zone to prevent looting. They were relieved by Maryland National Guard cavalry but later resumed their duties when cleanup began. MdHS

these rejected ballots, he still would have lost the election. The decision affirmed McLane's election as mayor, and he took office on May 19, 1903. [16]

Little more than a year later, and only three months after the fire, McLane married Mary van Bibber, a socially prominent and attractive widow from Philadelphia in a private ceremony in Washington. Reverend George C. Carter, a friend of McLane's, conducted the ceremony, held outside Baltimore in order to avoid the public sensation it would have caused in the city, given the young couple's celebrity. It was characteristic

of Robert McLane to avoid ostentation.

At the time of his marriage, McLane already had been enduring great stress for more than a year. The bitter primary race for the Democratic Party mayoral nomination and the contested election that followed it had drained much of his energy. His party had then refused to help him pay the court costs and other legal expenses in fighting Wachter's challenge to the election results, depressing him even more. The fire and its immediate aftermath consumed more of his energy. It is quite possible that his new wife did not recognize the signs of stress in her husband, who

Police officers, Secret Service, and firemen pose for a photograph at Pratt and Light Streets well after the fire has passed. MdHS

ABOVE: Detectives from New York, Philadelphia, Washington, York, Pennsylvania, and Baltimore pose before the ruined Herald building. MdHS

RIGHT: Detectives pose in the ruins. MdHS.

by the time they were married was enduring constant criticism from Baltimore's leading citizens. Among the final straws doubtless were the businessmen's incessant quarreling among themselves and with the administration about the widening of streets in the Burnt District and the impact this would have on the dimensions of their properties. Whatever may have been the combination of pressures and demands under which he labored, they crushed McLane.

Philadelphia socialite Mary van Bibber was married to Mayor Robert M. McLane a mere sixteen days before becoming a widow for the second time. From the *Baltimore News,* May 30, 1904. MdHS

The carriage ride from McLane's City Hall office to his home at 29 West Preston Street was less than a mile and took only a few minutes. On May 29, 1904, he arrived home apparently in good spirits, spoke briefly with Mary in their living room, then went upstairs, presumably to get ready for an outing with her. A noise startled Mary, who found her husband unconscious and near death on his bedroom floor from a single shot fired from his own pistol. The bullet had entered his right temple and come out behind his left ear. He died about three hours later without regaining consciousness. Conflicting theories soon appeared. It might not have been a suicide, some maintained, but an accidental discharge of his pearl-handled pistol, which was usually in a holster in one of his wardrobe drawers. Some maintained that McLane's fumbling through this drawer

E. Clay Timanus (left) was McLane's political rival and successor. He had blocked McLane's plans for reconstructing the city, but on McLane's suicide inherited them. MdHS

ABOVE:
South Calvert Street, cleaned of debris, looking north to the Maryland Trust and Continental Trust buildings, now gutted shells. The smaller red stone Mercantile Trust and Deposit Company sustained only minor damage. MdHS

FACING PAGE:
Alex. Brown Co., at the southwest corner of Baltimore and Calvert Streets survived the fire nearly intact. The Continental Trust across the street was, at sixteen stories, the tallest building in Baltimore, and the B&O Building next to Alex. Brown was eight stories tall. Miraculously, neither fell. MdHS

caused the pistol to fall to the floor and go off, but in time the weight of opinion shifted to suicide. Whichever reason underlay the tragedy, McLane had been married only sixteen days.

In accordance with the Baltimore City Charter, the president of the Second Branch of the City Council succeeded a fallen mayor. Republican E. Clay Timanus subsequently served the rest of McLane's term.

View looking north on
Charles Street from
Baltimore Street, after the
shells of buildings had
been pulled down. MdHS

143

Once McLane's fierce political opponent, Timanus now had no choice but to fight his battles.

Thomas O'Neill

Thomas O'Neill, successful merchant and owner of the dry goods store located at Charles and Lexington Streets, emerged as one of the most colorful characters of the Baltimore Fire. A hefty redhead, born in Cavan, Ireland, on November 19, 1849, O'Neill had come to Baltimore in 1866 and made his fortune by founding and expanding a store that many considered the most prestigious emporium of its kind south of Wanamaker's in Philadelphia. An engaging entrepreneur, he spent much of his time lavishing attention on customers and making sure that salespeople treated patrons courteously. O'Neill, an impressive six-footer, sported a red walrus mustache, pince-nez eyeglasses on a cord, a black frock coat with braided lapels, striped trousers, and a wing collar on his white shirt. Known to many on sight, O'Neill stood beside the door of his store each morning, welcoming customers.[17]

Founded as a linen shop in 1882, O'Neill's store grew in size and evolved into an early twentieth-century department store. It consisted of two buildings—an old four-story structure on the southwest corner of Charles and Lexington Streets, and a new six-story structure attached to the south side of the old building. O'Neill had prepared his store in the event of a fire. The interior had a Grinnell wet pipe sprinkler system utilizing 955 sprinkler heads. Outside, spray heads covered the eighty-six windows on the west side of the building.[18] Water for these sprinkler systems flowed freely from a ten-inch main on Lexington Street through an eight-inch fire service water connection. In addition, O'Neill's had a fifteen thousand-gallon water tank on the roof of the new building.

O'Neill had three overriding interests: his religion, his family, and the business. In fact, strong religious beliefs had a major influence on his actions during the Great Fire. News stories claim that on that fateful Sunday morning, O'Neill drove to the Carmelite Convent on Biddle Street and asked the nuns to pray for the safety of his store.[19] On returning to it, he found that some of his employees had arrived from home or church, and in an attempt to protect the store, had clogged the downspouts and smashed the water tank on the roof, releasing a large quantity of water. They hoped the resulting pool on the roof would be enough to extinguish any firebrands drifting onto it. O'Neill's men also stuffed blankets into the flues, cutting down on the draft that could spread a potential fire.

City dynamite crews on the mayor's orders were to clear fire lanes and block the further spread of the flames. As the fire approached O'Neill & Company, the dynamite team blew up two or three buildings on West Fayette Street, but instead of stopping the fire, the explosions seemed to expand it.

Thomas O'Neill. From *Men of Maryland,* 1905.

Around 7 P.M. on Sunday, the team placed explosives in the J. W. Putts & Company department store on the southwest corner of Fayette and Charles. The explosion on the Fayette Street side of the building shot fire-brands across the street into the Hall and Headington building on the northwest cor-ner. From there the fire advanced on Slessinger's Shoe Store, adjacent to O'Neill's new building. When the dynamite team arrived, O'Neill would not budge. He told the crew that if they tried to blow up his building, they "would have to blow him up with it."[20]

Courtesy Deutsche Bank
Alex. Brown

As flames advanced from the south and west, a windowless, solid firewall of bricks laid in cement protected the south side of O'Neill's store. His employees turned on the exterior sprinkler system on the west wall and sent a continuous shower of water cascading down the outside of the windows. A fire company on Charles Street protected the front of O'Neill's two buildings on the east. Despite these efforts, a portion of the cornice on the new building caught fire and ignited part of the roof. Fortunately, when it spread to the space between the roof and the ceiling on O'Neill's top floor, water spray from nine sprinkler heads extinguished it. O'Neill's preparations worked. The only damage amounted to the burned cornice, a partially burned water tank, and a few cracked show windows.

O'Neill's outside sprinkler system held the fire at bay until the wind shifted and placed the store out of danger. Quick thinking employees, a well-constructed building with a firewall, and windows protected by outside sprinklers helped save his livelihood, but in O'Neill's mind salvation had come from something greater. Asked over the years what saved his store, O'Neill responded, "his confidence and faith in providence." When he died in 1919, O'Neill left the Archdiocese of Baltimore $7 million. By 1956, two years after his store had closed for good, O'Neill's bequest had grown to $14 million, and the construction of the Cathedral of Mary Our Queen, completed in 1959, used $8.5 million of that legacy. An additional $3.5 million was allocated to construct Good Samaritan Hospital, a sum that had grown to $37 million by the time the hospital opened its doors in 1968.[21] Both owe much to a merchant who believed that Providence, more than sprinklers, saved his business from the Great Fire.

Edward B. Passano

Although a misfortune for many, the Baltimore Fire fostered a printing dynasty in that it gave Edward Boteler Passano (1872–1946) an opportunity to own the Williams & Wilkins printing business he had managed prior to the catastrophe.

In 1890, fourteen years before the fire, John H. Williams started a small printing business in the cellar of his house. Three years later, Henry B. (Harry) Wilkins joined Williams in establishing the Williams & Wilkins Company, which moved from 33 Post Office Avenue to 36 South Calvert Street. Williams provided a

View from the Shot Tower looking southwest shows the devastation from the Jones Falls on the left to Liberty Street on the far right with the basin as the southern boundary in the distance. MdHS

knowledge of the craft and general business management skills; Wilkins provided the capital, some of it his own, but the bulk loaned by his friends, bankers John W. and Robert Garrett. The young company grew, and by 1897 Williams & Wilkins hired a third person, Edward B. (Ned) Passano, twenty-five, a former classmate of Wilkins at Lehigh University, to sell their printing services. After Passano arrived, the company moved in 1898 to the old Klipper-Webster building located at 6 South Calvert Street. Passano took an active role in management and began to run the company two years later when his employers turned to other interests. According to a company history, "Wilkins left for Paris to study at the Sorbonne and Williams took a lucrative job in New York with the Columbia Graphaphone Company." With Ned Passano's hard work, the company

Edward B. Passano (ca. 1900) From *A Century of Progress 1890–1990* (Baltimore: Waverly Inc., 1989).

Remains of the Williams & Wilkins building. From *A Century of Progress 1890–1990* (Baltimore: Waverly Inc., 1989).

became so profitable that when Wilkins returned briefly from Paris, he bought out Williams' share of the stock and convinced the Garretts to join him in furnishing additional working capital. Leaving Passano to manage the business, Wilkins returned to

Paris and the company became "the largest and best known printing plant in the city," until the Great Fire of 1904.[22]

That Sunday morning, Ned Passano was in bed with the flu at his home in Towson. Learning about the fire early in the afternoon,

Baltimore Street looking north. From left, the court house, post office, customs house, and City Hall, all survived the fire. MdHS

he struggled out of his sickbed and hurried the ten miles downtown on a horse-drawn streetcar. He met briefly with a number of employees in front of the company's building at 6 South Charles Street, who then attempted to gather up what they could as the raging fire moved toward them. They saved two truckloads of bookplates from the fifth floor of the building by moving them to the cellar of a foreman's house. Lack of transportation prevented their taking more materials out of harm's way, so workers moved more bookplates to a vault in the company's basement,

hoping that they would survive. The heavy plates had to be moved by hand because the elevator transported them only to street level. Workers then had to carry them around the building to another entrance and down to the vault in the basement. The hastily assembled crew raced to save things of value, including company records, but before they had finished the electricity failed, the fire neared, and the police ordered everyone out of the building. Although the fire destroyed the company's building and ruined its machinery and equipment beyond repair, the items secured in the

vaults survived, preserving the bookplates intended for their largest customer.

Some businesses never recovered from the fire, but Passano boldly led the Williams & Wilkins Company's resurgence. As luck would have it, two carloads of paper enroute to Passano arrived in Baltimore after the fire, ensuring an ample supply of that basic printers' commodity.[23] Passano's defining moment came when he established operations in borrowed spaces and coordinated efforts to fill printing orders in the immediate wake of the fire. Despite the scarcity of space, Williams & Wilkins was printing within a week, on borrowed presses in four plants scattered about the city, setting type in two widely separated lofts, and issuing orders from a business office in still another building. Using binding services in Philadelphia and New York, the company delivered finished products to its largest customer, the H. M. Rowe Company, a business school publisher, within two weeks of the fire. Passano accomplished all of this in a city where normal services were crippled and he was bidding against dozens of other companies for facilities and space.

THE GREAT
BALTIMORE
FIRE

As more citizens were permitted into the district, businessmen came to inspect the ruins of their firms—and those of their competitors. Panorama after most of the smoke has settled and many of the buildings have been pulled down. MdHS

154 ☙

FACING PAGE: Because of their weight, safes, in many cases, crashed through burning floors. Removing them from the rubble required strong backs, makeshift ramps, and leverage. MdHS

BELOW: Some foundations could be reused, but first debris had to be extracted. MdHS

THE GREAT
BALTIMORE
FIRE

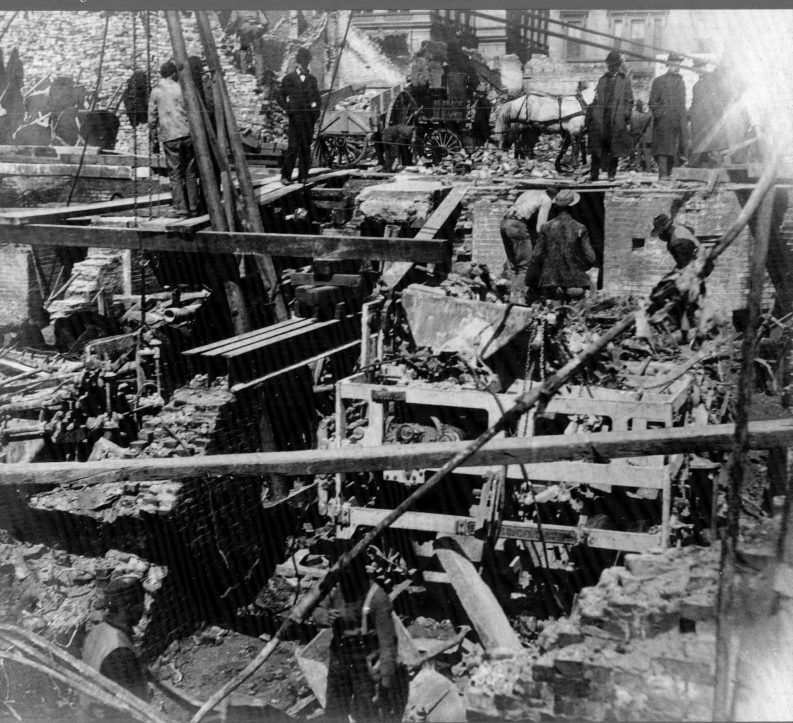

Some of the characters moving safes seem more interesting than the valuable contents. MdHS

Reminiscent of a comic skit by Eddie Foy—the headline performer during Chicago's Iroquois Theatre Fire six weeks earlier—a police officer and a well-dressed gentleman pose next to a safe. Note the clothesbasket containing charred paper. MdHS

After streets were cleared, and buildings stripped of everything valuable, the next step was to bring down unstable
walls. At first they attempted to do so with dynamite, but
later resorted to pulling walls down with cables attached to
steam engines. MdHS

Workers initially used
dynamite to collapse the
walls of destroyed build-
ings. Although the method
seems to have worked in
this case, many times it
simply blew holes in the
ground. Early in the
reconstruction of the city,
steam engines and men
with hooks and cables
pulled down derelict walls
rather than resorting to
dynamite. Enoch Pratt
Free Library

*Blowing up Bldg with
dinamite on Balto St.*

Men use a cable to pull
down a wall.
Library of Congress

Construction begins in this view of the Burnt District just west of Charles Street. The irrepressible Thomas O'Neill has a freshly painted sign on the side of his store. Note the water tank on O'Neill's roof, which helped save the building. Governor Warfield's Fidelity Deposit & Trust Company is just visible behind O'Neill's. MdHS

An improvised railway on
Charles between German
and Lombard Streets to
haul away rubble. MdHS

Center Market Space from Pratt St. looking N.

Construction underway
at the Center Market at
Pratt Street looking north.
MdHS

 163

The intersection of Baltimore and Charles Streets bus-
tles with activity approximately three weeks after the
fire. The tall building at left is the Calvert Building at
Fayette and St. Paul Streets. MdHS

Trolleys were once again operating on Baltimore Street, and construction was soon underway. MdHS

Balto & South Sts. Looking N.E.

Clearing and repairing building foundations at Baltimore and South Streets, looking northeast. MdHS

Construction is well along on Baltimore Street. The Number 17 Route car is traveling west along a damaged roadbed. MdHS

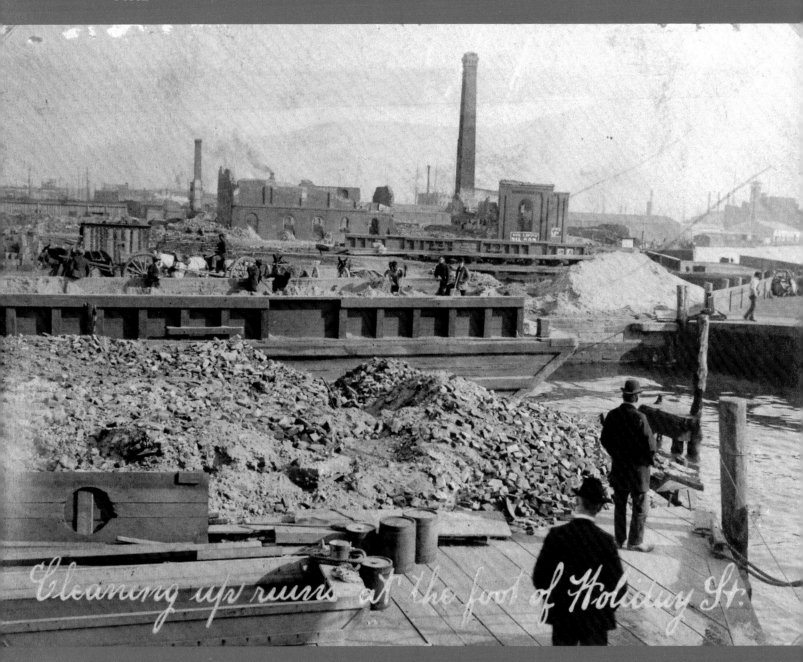

Cleaning up ruins at the foot of Holliday St.

Loading debris onto barges
at the foot of Holliday
Street. MdHS

Balto St. looking E. from Charles St.

Repairing Baltimore
Street. MdHS

Remains of the Maryland
Institute at Harrison and
Baltimore Streets. MdHS

Clearing debris at Hanover
and Lombard Streets.
MdHS

Hopkins' Losses

THE GREAT FIRE'S DEVASTATION affected even some major Baltimore institutions that never directly felt the flames. The Johns Hopkins Hospital — located ten blocks east of the Burnt District and far from harm's way — nevertheless lost its major source of endowment income because the blaze destroyed sixty-eight buildings in downtown Baltimore that were owned by the hospital. In fact, "Hopkins Hospital was one of the greatest losers of buildings, including valuable warehouses, stores, and other structures."[1] Although the hospital's landmark, domed building on North Broadway in East Baltimore was unharmed, the value of its investment properties totaled about $1,300,000. Fortunately, fire insurance compensated for much of the destruction, with the net loss to Hopkins Hospital being approximately $500,000. Luckily, John D. Rockefeller, then beginning his multiple benefi-cences, bestowed a gift of $500,000 on Hopkins to cover the losses.[2]

Hopkins still faced the challenge of replacing the $65,000 in annual income it had derived from the lost sixty-eight buildings. Combined with $35,000 received "from the rental of other property in control of the trustees," this money had been used to cover the medical expenses of impov-erished patients who were admitted free to the hospital.[3]

Daniel Coit Gilman, who had been the first president of Hopkins, attended numerous meetings of city officials and business leaders and along with other prominent members of the community helped Baltimore snap back from this tragedy. Writing to Minton Warren, a former Latin professor at Hopkins who had moved on to Harvard, Gilman observed, "There is no whining so far as I can see but a feeling that there is work to be done and that we must take hold and do it."[4]

Voicing his sympathy for the loss of Hopkins' endowment properties, Warren wrote to Gilman's successor, Hopkins president Ira Remsen, on February 13, 1904, "I am sorry to see that the university has met with some direct losses in buildings from which it is deriving an income."[5]

The Johns Hopkins University, then located in various buildings near Monument and Howard Streets, also escaped damage from the Great Fire. Closer to downtown than the hospital, its buildings were located eight blocks north of the Burnt District and never felt a spark.

---

[1] *The Baltimore Sun Almanac for 1905,* 1905, January 1, p. 76.

[2] Clautice, Joseph W. "The Great Fire of February 7, 1904," *Baltimore,* January 1954, p. 25.

[3] *The Baltimore Sun Almanac for 1905,* 1905, January 1, p. 76.

[4] Letter from former Hopkins president Daniel Coit Gilman to Minton Warren, former Hopkins associate professor and then Latin professor at Harvard, February 9, 1904. Daniel Gilman Papers, MS1 Box 1.50, Coutesy of Special Collections, Sheridan Libraries, The Johns Hopkins University.

[5] Letter from Minton Warren to Hopkins president Ira Remsen, February 13, 1904. Remsen Papers, MS39 Box 4, Courtesy of Special Collections, Sheridan Libraries, The Johns Hopkins University.

Robert Garrett (ca. 1904)
From *A Century of Progress
1890–1990* (Baltimore:
Waverly Inc., 1989).

In the midst of these feverish efforts to save the company, Passano received a cable from Harry Wilkins in Paris directing him to "collect the insurance, pay off the Garretts, and liquidate the business."[24] After seven years of hard work making the business profitable, Passano was not going to give up now. Nevertheless, as the majority stockholder Wilkins had every right to pay off the loan from the Garrett brothers and close down the business. John Garrett was traveling abroad and not available, but in an attempt to save the company, Passano met with banker Robert Garrett, who as a member of the Maryland Cavalry was on duty with his unit in the fire zone. In a stable on Calvert Street at the edge of the fire zone, Passano convinced Robert Garrett that Williams & Wilkins should continue.[25] When John Garrett returned to Baltimore, the brothers agreed with Passano's plan to purchase the business in two phases. First, the Garretts would compensate Wilkins in cash and with

The Williams & Wilkins
Company building on
Greenmount Avenue, 1910.
The Williams & Wilkins
Company, *Three-Quarters
of a Century Plus Ten,
1890–1975* (Baltimore:
Waverly Press, 1975).

notes signed by Passano. Then, after Passano had used profits from the business to pay the notes to Wilkins, he would purchase the Garretts' share of the business by issuing additional notes, this time payable to the Garretts. In 1907, Ned Passano paid off the last of these notes and finally owned Williams & Wilkins.

Even before the Great Fire, it was clear that downtown Baltimore had to modernize from its outgrown colonial infrastructure and haphazard expansion during the three decades following the Civil War. Although Baltimore had been the second largest city in the nation in 1850, it no longer held that honor, or the distinction of being the gateway to the South.[26] In addition, until the late 1890s Baltimore's political temperament tended to be conservative, reflecting the gloom of the terrible economic depression of 1893 and the bitterness remaining from the Civil War, in which Baltimoreans had divided their loyalties and still distrusted some of their neighbors.

Members of the Civil War generation still dominated Baltimore society, resulting in a cautious response to younger voices and a reluctance to undertake municipal improvements. Although some recognized the need to modernize, it seemed impossible for community leaders to marshal the necessary support and willingness to sacrifice.

In 1895 progressive reformers finally gained control of Baltimore by overcoming a political machine that had been firmly entrenched since 1871. Reformers established a new city charter in 1898 that streamlined the city's organizational structure and gave it a government similar to that of the United States. It now had a bicameral legislative body consisting of two independent houses called a First and Second Branch of the City Council and an executive, the mayor. The mayor, a genuine executive and administrator with the power to appoint, could determine the policies of the city and set its course. The city council, actually a local legislature, had the power to pass ordinances subject to limitations declared in the city charter.[27] Both the First and Second Branches of the City Council had to approve public improvements, which posed a serious problem since constituents differed on how Baltimore should rebuild its central business district. Adding to the difficulties of the legislative process, results of the last election placed the Democrats in control of the First Branch while the Republicans controlled the Second Branch.[28] As might be expected, measures championed by one branch of the council often met disapproval in the other.

Politically split and frequently opposed by Republican and Democratic political machines that continued to rule Maryland politics statewide, reformers had largely failed in their attempts at redevelopment. Now faced with the tragic and significant destruction of the Great Fire, Progressives hoped that Baltimore's city government would prevail over the private and often self-serving interests that had long stood in the way of needed improvements in public infrastructure. Unfortunately, that did not occur during McLane's administration.

Prior to the fire, narrow streets and a maze of often crooked or dead-end roads had congested downtown traffic. Unlike major cities in Europe and the United States, Baltimore had no expansive boulevards with majestic buildings. Instead, builders created newer and more substantial buildings amidst older ones, creating a blend of uncomplimentary shapes with little aesthetic charm.

Buildings near the harbor basin tended to be old and in some cases rotted and used for purposes other than originally intended. An array of utility poles for trolley car, electrical, telephone, and telegraph wires further narrowed the streets. Workers often installed new wires without removing the old ones until a tangled, black network of wires hung above the streets and sidewalks like an ungainly blanket. To reduce the number of overhead wires, construction of underground conduits began in February 1901, but by 1904 workers had relieved only a few blocks, removing only 230 of the thousands of utility poles located downtown.[29]

Baltimore's wastewater system also was primitive. Privies emptied into cesspools that in many cases flowed downhill in old streambeds to the harbor basin and the Jones Falls. In time, stone arches had covered many of the old streambeds, which in some cases oozed under buildings on their way to the harbor. Although prohibited by law, raw sewage often emptied into storm drains that flowed south, too. The result was predictable. Sanitary conditions were awful, and the stench from the harbor brought out the best of Baltimore's black humor. The last major change in the harbor basin, sometimes called the "back basin" by health professionals, had occurred in the 1820s when workers filled in the northern portion, permitting Pratt and Lombard Streets to extend all the way east to the Jones Falls. Builders constructed wharves and piers for waterfront businesses and industries, but with an undesirable result: by 1904 the dredges needed to remove accumulated silt in the harbor would not fit into the narrow docks, and the area was soon unsuitable for shipping. Baltimore's waterfront badly needed modernization to participate in the commerce of the early twentieth century.[30]

Although it appeared that Baltimore was politically unable to enact the necessary reforms to modernize the city, some members of the community did take progressive action. In January 1904, Richard M. Venable, president of the Board of Park Commissioners, Theodore Marburg, organizer of the Municipal Arts Society, William Keyser, Supervisor of City Charities, and representatives from three business and improvement associations supported a bill for public improvements in Baltimore. The Baltimore Board of Estimates approved the loan on February 2, and on February 6, 1904, Baltimore's delegation to the General Assembly indicated its readiness to support bills to provide the city with the necessary funds for street paving, schools, sewers, parks, and fire houses. Although the Great Fire over the next two days would alter many of these plans for improvement, massive changes ultimately would occur.

Efforts at developing a far-reaching, progressive plan to rebuild downtown Baltimore began on Tuesday February 9, the day after firefighters brought the fire under control. Meeting in the home of progressive reformer and businessman William Keyser, leaders of Baltimore's business and financial communities discussed needed reforms in the city's infrastructure, including the widening of streets in the central business district. A recommendation arose during this meeting that Mayor McLane appoint a committee of prominent citizens to consider the planning of the city's reconstruction and advise him accordingly. On the same day, leaders of insurance companies met and organized the General Loss Committee to expedite the resolution of claims. Chaired by Paul Turner, this committee of representatives from affected insurance companies agreed to establish an office at the Royal Arcanum building, across the street from the Rennert Hotel. A notice in the newspapers advised the public of the committee's purpose and invited anyone with questions about their fire insurance claims to contact them without charge. Turner developed a procedure for dealing with the public, staffed the office with fifteen clerks to process claims, and sorted out many of the situations when claimants had fire insurance coverage from several companies.[31]

The street cleaning commission expanded its earlier operations with a major effort on Thursday, February 11, involving about three thousand workers.[32] Divided into small groups, each with an appointed leader, the street cleaners walked into the Burnt District and began to clear the major roads. While they initially threw debris to the side of the road, they later used horse-drawn wagons to remove rubble picked up in the streets. National banks reestablished their offices in temporary locations and opened their doors to the public on Friday, February 12, enabling commerce and industry to regain some of their financial services. On the same day, while isolated structures continued to burn, McLane appointed a sixty-three member Citizen's Emergency Committee in response to the proposal developed at William Keyser's home on Tuesday. This advisory committee considered reconstruction problems and developed recommendations concerning the rebuilding of the Burnt District. McLane chose Keyser to chair this committee, ensuring that someone with progressive ideals would lead the rebuilding of downtown. Keyser divided this group of prominent citizens into subcommittees to consider and make recommendations concerning reconstruction, legislation, financing, and the improvement of the network of Baltimore's streets.[33]

On Saturday afternoon, President Theodore Roosevelt sent his eldest daughter Alice, a vivacious personality in her own right, to view the devastation and transmit his good will and sympathy to the citizens. Wanting to dash over to Baltimore and help fight the fire himself on the first day, Roosevelt had wisely held back and stayed out of the way, thereby avoiding the confusion associated with a presidential visit. General Riggs met Alice Roosevelt at the court house. He promptly waived the rule prohibiting women in the Burnt District and permitted her to tour it in a carriage with a collapsible top. Traveling along Fayette Street with the top down, Alice Roosevelt had a clear view of the devastation. On reaching the western edge of the Burnt District, she could look south and view the spot where the fire started three blocks away.

While demolition crews dynamited or pulled down unstable walls and the remains of dilapidated buildings, the Citizen's Emergency Committee settled down from their initial bursts of enthusiasm and proceeded to the complex issues concerning reconstruction and reform of Baltimore's infrastructure. The subcommittee on street improvements, meeting at Theodore Marburg's house, developed two major objectives. One plan would reduce the congestion of east-west traffic that funneled onto Baltimore and Pratt Streets; the second would eliminate bottlenecks in the narrow streets with heavy traffic in the western portion of the Burnt District. On the advice of Frederick Law Olmsted Jr., son of the writer and landscape architect, the subcommittee proposed that builders widen eleven major streets in the Burnt District.[34] Further following Olmsted's suggestions, the subcommittee recommended that the city purchase the harbor basin wharf area and construct an

attractive system of docks, wharves, and piers that could accommodate modern shipping needs. Other recommendations by this subcommittee included smooth-paving of streets, establishing a park in Marsh Market, laying sewer connections for a future citywide sewer system, and limiting the height of buildings constructed in the future to one hundred fifty feet. To finance these structural improvements, estimated to cost $9 million, officials planned to utilize the $4 million in proceeds from the city's earlier sale of Western Maryland Railroad stock, which had been set aside to build sewers. The balance of $5 million would come from a bond issue.

On Monday, February 15, saloons and bars reopened with a warning to patrons that the Board of Police Commissioners would close the taverns in the event of breaches of peace and order. That Monday, Richard Venable, chair of the subcommittee on legislation, also proposed the creation of a Burnt District Commission to supervise the reconstruction of the devastated area. The very active and productive Citizens' Emergency Committee and its subcommittees met daily from February 12–22, when it adjourned. McLane accepted its wide range of recommendations and persuaded the General Assembly to pass an enabling act on March 11 giving him the authority to appoint a bipartisan Burnt District Commission consisting of himself, two Republicans, and two Democrats. This Burnt District Commission could initiate legislation to implement the recommendations of the Citizen's Emergency Committee.

Appointed and confirmed by the Second Branch of the City Council on March 12, the commission went about its business without consulting leaders in the business community or the public in general. Because the commis-

Baltimore's mayor
Robert M. Mclane

sion's decisions could have significant impact, opposition quickly arose. Listening to property owners on Baltimore Street who objected to its widening because that would make their properties smaller, the Republican-dominated Second Branch of the City Council increased its opposition to McLane's street-widening plans. Baltimore's Board of Estimates then rejected Olmsted's plan for construction of a recreational pier and a park at Marsh Market. Nevertheless, revitalization of the harbor continued, with the city condemning and taking over the northern portion of the basin.

Mayor E. Clay Timanus

Following McLane's suicide, E. Clay Timanus, a Republican and opponent of much of McLane's efforts, found himself having to continue the work McLane had started. Timanus had led the effort by the Second Branch to defeat five of the Burnt District Commission's proposed street improvements, but now he championed the fight for their approval. Two major obstacles stood in the way of citywide improvements. First, the legislature had to pass enabling legislation, and second, voters had to concur with the financing by voting for necessary bond issues. Timanus was fortunate in having two astute advisors, Solicitor Bruce Gaither and his brother George Gaither, who succeeded Timanus as president of the Second Branch. With their help, Timanus created a forum to bring together all segments of

J. Barry Mahool succeeded Timanus. MdHS

the community to jointly participate in planning for the reconstruction and revitalization of Baltimore.

With the wider participation of citizens and businessmen previously avoided by the quick (but sometimes failed) actions of the Burnt District Commission, Timanus accomplished much. His vehicle for this collaboration was the Greater Public Improvements Conference that he assembled in December 1904. Delegates came from almost all parts of the city as did representatives of business and industrial interests. One major group not represented, reflecting the era's strict segregation, was Baltimore's African American community. Following the conference, officials closely allied with Timanus assigned priorities to the various public improvements, and an election referendum in May 1905 included proposals for funding three major initiatives. One called for a $10 million sewer improvement loan; the second sought a $1 million loan for parks; and the third requested a $2 million dollar loan for street improvements, a topographical survey, small bridge construction, and an extension of street cleaning and garbage collection activities to newer parts of the city. Bipartisan political support promoted the ratification of these bond issues, enabling Mayor Timanus to achieve what McLane had attempted earlier but failed to accomplish.

Although Timanus and McLane before him had made considerable progress in modernizing Baltimore's crumbling public infrastructure, the progressive reform envisioned by Venable, Marburg, and Keyser prior to the Great Fire did not entirely materialize following the blaze. Urban renewal and a total structural reform would be attempted again in Baltimore during the administration of Franklin D. Roosevelt, and repeatedly during the second half of the twentieth century.

⇜ Epilogue ⇝

THE GREAT BALTIMORE FIRE consumed more than 140 acres—seventy blocks—containing over fifteen hundred buildings and four lumberyards in downtown Baltimore. Raging beyond control for thirty hours, it burned out more than twenty-five hundred businesses and ruined many of their owners financially. In a city of 539,000 people, it threw about thirty-five thousand out of work. For all its vast, destructive power, the fire caused only one reported death, and no serious injuries.

Within two years, most of Baltimore's businesses had moved from their cramped, temporary quarters to impressive, reconstructed buildings, and commerce had returned to its prosperous routine. Baltimore had snapped back from the brink of ruin. Visitors in 1906 called the reconstruction unbelievable and miraculous. Photographs of the renewed district did not show that Baltimore still lacked a sewer system, or that it remained one of the last major cities to modernize its approach for dealing with wastewater. A renovated high-pressure water distribution system and conduits for electrical, telephone, and telegraph wires were also longer in coming. Still, on the surface, the rebuilt city seemed stunning. Larger, more modern buildings replaced those

the fire had destroyed. About eight hundred buildings valued at approximately $25 million replaced fourteen hundred smaller, brick buildings assessed at about $13 million before the fire. Five of the city's steel-frame skyscrapers, although burned internally, remained structurally sound, allowing owners to gut the buildings down to their framework and rebuild. With those and a few other exceptions, the majority of the new brick structures rose only three and four stories high. By widening streets, the city acquired nearly ten additional acres of street space, and it gained twenty-eight acres of docks and markets with the revitalization of the harbor and market areas.[1] All told, the city spent more than $7 million rebuilding docks and streets. Assessments to property owners adjacent to these areas yielded $1.1 million toward paying for the improvements.

One result of all this construction was a depletion of capital that had long-term effects on modernization projects previously planned by individual firms and the city itself. Baltimore's refusal of outside financial assistance exacerbated the shortage. Mayor McLane's polite but immediate refusal of monetary aid was in keeping with the times: people considered it inappropriate for a proud city like Baltimore to accept "hand outs" or charity. Baltimore therefore accomplished all of its rebuilding without assistance of any kind, including federal or state subsidies.

Still, they had accomplished more than anyone anticipated. Jubilee Week, September 9–16, 1906, celebrated Baltimore's recovery from the Great Fire and provided the perfect opportunity to present the new city to the world. Municipal pride was on prominent display in a series of parades, particularly one on September 13 to honor firefighters, who marched and rode past cheering crowds. About fourteen hundred firefighters participated, including almost all of Baltimore's department and many from departments near and far who had come to help battle the Great Fire. Among the marchers was the most popular animal in Maryland—Goliath—the horse that had become a hero by diverting its

The fire horse, Goliath, became a local equine celebrity. In the first minutes of the fire, he veered sharply to avoid flames reaching from the Hurst building and in so doing saved his team, a Hale Water Tower, and several firemen from a collapsing wall. Note the burn scars on his neck and right hindquarter. MdHS

Hale Water Tower, human crew, and other horses from being crushed on Liberty Street by a falling wall from the Hurst building. Covered with garlands, Goliath pranced by the reviewing stands, appearing to understand and appreciate the crowd's wild ovation.

More than half a century later, Benjamin W. Weaver, who retired as deputy chief of Washington's fire department, recalled participating in Baltimore's thank-you parade as a sergeant in No. 2 Engine Company. Weaver's group rose early to load fifteen horses in a boxcar and five engines on flatcars at Union Station in the District. Firefighters themselves rode in a coach, and the contingent arrived at Camden Station at about 10 A.M., looking crisp and ready for a parade ground inspection, men, horses, and engines. By noon, however, they were feeling the heat of what seemed like the hottest day of the year. (The weather service recorded a high temperature of eighty-eight degrees.) Weaver and his colleagues felt fortunate to be wearing only caps, while some of the participants in other units wore much heavier, and hotter, helmets. Weaver noticed that the fire commissioners

Lexington Street looking west. Note the narrow width of the street. In the distance at top right is the Fidelity Deposit & Trust Company Building on Charles Street.
Enoch Pratt Free Library

looked uncomfortable in their frock coats, striped pants, and tall, silk hats. Although the parade was scheduled to start at 2 P.M., another unit had difficulty unloading in the rail yard and delayed the start. Heat overcame one Washington firefighter, Frank Clements, as his company formed up for the march.

Eventually the parade got under way. Starting from South Broadway, the procession turned left onto East Baltimore Street and marched west toward City Hall. Passing in review, many of the participants from out of town did not recognize Governor Edwin Warfield and Mayor E. Clay Timanus on the reviewing stand, and Weaver recalled that a group of boys heckled those who did not tip their hats to the dignitaries. The parade passed through the rejuvenated Burnt District, then turned right on Howard Street and marched up to Monument Street and across to Mount Vernon Place, where it broke up.

Horses particularly felt the heat during the march, and the parade stopped from time to time to cool them and give them water. At the conclusion of the parade, many of the out-of-town units remained for a large celebration that evening at Electric Park, near

A Jubilee ticket. Courtesy, Wayne Schaumburg.

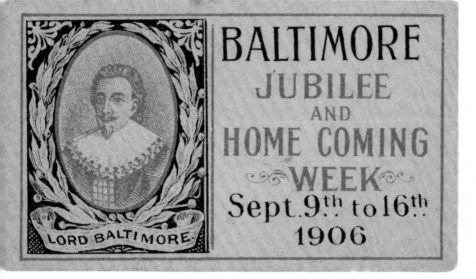

Pimlico Race Track. The city provided streetcars to take them there. The Washingtonians, who were scheduled to participate in another parade in the capital, moved on to the rail yard for their scheduled return home by 6 P.M. A delay in loading equipment caused a much later departure, and they did not get back to Union Station until around eleven that night. Although Washington went through the motions, not much of a parade occurred in the District due to the late hour and the condition of the horses. The Washington detachment had suffered no casualties during the Great Fire, but the celebration was another matter. In addition to the firefighter overcome by the heat in Baltimore, four of the unit's horses died from the heat after they returned to the capital.[2]

Baltimore's Jubilee Week occurred at a time when many cities in the United States had homecoming events to encourage their citizens' municipal pride and to foster economic development and commerce. A surviving ticket to the Baltimore celebration has a sketch of Lord Baltimore on the left and the words "Baltimore Jubilee and Home Coming Week Sept. 9th to 16th 1906." Six months earlier a newspaper had described the upcoming event as the "Greater Baltimore Jubilee and Exposition," and suggested that merchants use Center Market Space to display products. As it happened, emphasis shifted from an exhibition of goods to exuberant celebrations honoring firefighters, and much eating and drinking.

Following the success of Baltimore's Jubilee, the entire state of Maryland had a similar event thirteen months later. Titled "Maryland's Home-Coming Week," it occurred in Baltimore October 13–19, 1907. A lengthy, bound official program displayed a photograph of a rotund, white-haired, mustachioed, and goateed Governor Warfield, who also served as president of the Home-Coming Association.[3] Six of the seven days of this precisely organized, weeklong event took place in Baltimore. The seventh featured excursions to Annapolis by boat and rail. With the exception of "church day," each day included parades with marching bands—forty on one occasion—and numerous floats. Baltimore's new mayor in 1907, J. Barry Mahool, had prominent roles in these celebrations. The program included a lengthy discussion of the Great Fire and the city's recovery. Contemporary news clippings and photos of the 1907 Maryland Home-Coming indicate that in scale and spirit it matched the Baltimore Jubilee in 1906.

Baltimore and Maryland had arrived in the modern era in a most dramatic manner, but there was still much work to be done. In response to the Great Fire, the fire department increased the number of firefighters and horses by half, and newly installed hydrants and alarm boxes provided necessary coverage for an expanding urban area. The installation of a high-pressure water service covered seventy additional acres of the city.

Concurrent with necessary and long overdue municipal reforms, Baltimoreans had to cope with other changes in their lives. The introduction of the automobile affected Maryland greatly, with the number of vehicles increasing from about ten at the turn of the century to approximately ten thousand in

AFTER—Looking west from St. Paul & Baltimore Streets. MdHS

1914.[4] Baltimore dealers along Mount Royal Avenue near Pennsylvania Station (constructed in 1911), north of downtown, included Peerless, the Hupmobile, Chalmers, the Locomobile, Hudson, the Riordan, Packard, Pathfinder, the Kissel-Kar, and Cadillac. Other dealers sold less expensive models along North Avenue.[5] Traffic soon clogged the roads, as Baltimore became a way station for motorists traveling between New York and Washington, D.C. Long-distance travelers driving automobiles packed downtown streets recently widened to relieve horse-drawn traffic congestion. In 1906 work began on a boulevard connecting Washington and Baltimore.

Builders completed a small sewerage pilot plant at Walbrook in 1906, and with great ceremony the full-size Back River plant came on line in 1909. The mayor and members of the city council celebrated its inaugural by driving through a portion of the huge sewer in new, open touring cars. The sewers relieved Baltimore's alleys of frozen wastewater that could not drain during the winter months. Construction of underground conduits for sewers, a high-pressure water system, and electrical wires required extensive coordination, excavation, and careful mapping to record their precise locations, work that took about ten years after the fire to accomplish. Moving wires underground removed a serious impediment to future firefighters. No longer would overhead wires stop ladders and water

towers, or diffuse streams of water that firemen propelled toward the flames. Workers replaced the six-inch water mains with much larger mains, ranging from ten inches to forty inches in diameter and laid approximately 150 miles of new gas mains and extended steam pipes to buildings throughout downtown.[6]

Progressive reformers as well as Baltimore's middle-class voters supported candidates who pledged to work toward improving education, cleanliness, and order. Democrat James H. Preston won the Baltimore mayoral race in 1911 and completed work on Baltimore's sewer system and a water filtration plant at Lake Montebello. Preston championed amendments to the city's charter that modernized and reformed Baltimore's civil service system and established a unicameral city council.[7] In the summer of 1912, Baltimore fittingly gained national attention when the Democratic Party nominated Woodrow Wilson as its presidential candidate in the Fifth Regiment Armory. Baltimore was at last a city fully in step with the new twentieth century.

BEFORE AND AFTER:
Looking north from
Lombard Street and
Hopkins Place after the
fire and two years later.
MdHS

186

BEFORE AND AFTER:
North from Lombard and
Charles Streets. MdHS

BEFORE AND AFTER:
East from Calvert and
Baltimore Streets.
MdHS

Baltimore had its share of remarkable individuals during the Great Fire. Afterward, some experienced good fortune and personal success, while others were less fortunate.

Lewin H. Burkhardt (1867–1930)

As Fifth District Engineer, Burkhardt led the initial response to the Hurst building, where the fire started. On March 3, 1912, he became Deputy Chief Engineer of the Baltimore City Fire Department until New Year's Day 1922, when he assumed the role of Deputy Chief for the First Division. Lewin died on November 11, 1930, while serving in this position.

August Emrich (1863–1945)

August Emrich who acted as chief engineer after Horton's evacuation, enjoyed a full career as Baltimore's fire chief from 1912 to 1932. Among other things, Emrich supervised the motorization and modernization of the department. Placed on the pension roll on November 15, 1932, he retired at the age of sixty-nine. After fifty years with the fire department, Emrich attended a joyful farewell party at a friend's house on Johnson Street. "I feel like a caged bird that suddenly has been freed," he declared, when relieved from his responsibilities after two decades.[8]

Robert Garrett (1875–1961)

Robert Garrett represented his prominent and wealthy family with distinction. In addition to his academic achievements, Olympic officials proclaimed him champion discus thrower of the world at the first revival of the Olympic Games in Athens in 1896. As a member of Cavalry Troop A of the Maryland National Guard for seven years, he rose to the modest rank of corporal, and it was in this capacity at age twenty-eight that he served Baltimore during and after the fire. In addition to being a successful banker and businessman, throughout his long life his philanthropies were numerous and beneficial.[9]

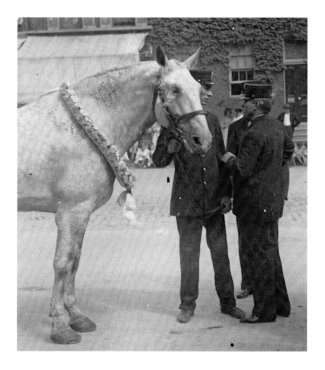

Goliath

After saving himself, his firefighters, other horses, and a Hale Water Tower by pulling them out from under the falling walls of the Hurst building, Goliath became the most famous animal in Maryland. Seared by the flames on his right side, Goliath received the best of care, and when he recovered appeared as the bright star in numerous parades and fairs. The city council by special act gave him a lifetime position in the Baltimore Fire Department, thereby sparing him the fate of other fire horses that became workhorses in other city departments or were sold or destroyed at the end of their firefighting service.[10]

Charles H. Grasty (1863–1924)

Less than four months after Grasty moved the *Evening News* into a makeshift plant at an abandoned foundry on February 28, 1904, he began work on a seven-story plant in the heart of Baltimore, at the southeast corner of Calvert and Fayette Streets. A large window on the first floor facing Calvert Street drew the attention of passersby as the presses ran.[11] Charles Grasty, a man of action, continued at a fast pace. Within a few years of the fire he became the editor of the *Sun*. In that capacity, he founded the *Evening Sun* as a direct rival to his former paper. He also became an early and influential supporter of Woodrow Wilson. When Wilson considered leaving the presidency of Princeton University, Grasty offered him the job as editor of the *Sun*. Instead, Wilson ran for governor of New Jersey and won. When the Democrats held their nominating convention in Baltimore in 1912, Grasty published front-page editorials supporting Wilson, who later that year won election to the office of President of the United States.

George W. Horton (1846–1920)

Succeeding Chief William C. McAfee on May 21, 1901, Horton served as chief of Baltimore's fire department during a number of Democratic and Republican administrations until placed on the pension roll March 2, 1912. Enjoying the respect and confidence of his subordinates, Horton went out of his way to remain free from partisanship, and enjoyed the respect of fellow chief engineers throughout the nation who often asked for his council and advice.[12]

William Keyser (1835–1904)

Although active and successful in business and industry, William Keyser always found time to help improve the lives of people in the community. As a leader in progressive reform efforts that were gaining momentum at the time of the fire, he often found himself swimming against political tides. Not reluctant to oppose his fellow corporate executives, Keyser focused much of his time and energy on trying to rehabilitate Baltimore after the fire. Unfortunately, on June 3, less than four months after the fire, he was stricken with "apoplexy" during an outdoor walk and died immediately.[13]

William C. McAfee (1865–1906)

When told that he would not be reinstated chief of the fire department when his term expired on June 4, 1901, William McAfee tendered his resignation. Apparently, his personal relationship with Mayor Hayes had been a difficult one. At the time of his resignation, the *Sun* opposed Hayes and sided with McAfee. Although Mayor McLane asked him to help during the Great Fire after Horton's injury, the press exaggerated McAfee's assistance; indeed, he was not a leader during the blaze. However, on February 16, 1904, a week after the fire, Governor Warfield appointed the popular McAfee state fire marshal.

Mayor Robert M. McLane (1867–1904)

The mayor of Baltimore from May 19, 1903 to May 30, 1904, McLane apparently died by his own hand after leading the effort to control the fire but finding difficulty and great stress during the aftermath. He married Mrs.

Mary van Bibber on May 14, 1904, sixteen days before he died.[14]

Henry Louis Mencken (1880–1956)

H. L. Mencken followed his remarkable performance as the young city editor of a major paper during Baltimore's greatest catastrophe by becoming one of America's most popular and controversial writers. In addition to writing thousands of newspaper columns, he contributed chapters to more than twenty books and wrote approximately thirty of his own. Some have argued that he wrote mainly for himself. One reporter claimed to have observed Mencken during an unguarded moment typing a column. After clacking out a sentence or two, Mencken read them over, roared with laughter, and slapped his sides.

Thomas O'Neill (1849–1919)

O'Neill's store, probably the most exclusive south of Wanamaker's in Philadelphia, continued to prosper after the fire, and his fortune grew. Appreciative of the divine powers that he claimed saved his store, O'Neill left a $7 million dollar bequest to the Archdiocese of Baltimore, specifically for the building of the Cathedral of Mary Our Queen. Other bequests went to Good Samaritan Hospital.[15]

Edward B. Passano (1872–1946)

Edward "the Skipper" Passano positioned his company to become one of the world's foremost publishers of scientific and medical books, periodicals, and electronic media. Reassembled in a part of Baltimore formerly known as the village of Waverly, the company became known as "the Waverly Press," a name later adapted for printing operations, while the title of "Williams & Wilkins" represented the company's publishing efforts. Eventually the company would call all of these endeavors "Waverly Inc," now located in historic Camden Yards adjacent to Oriole Park. The Passano family owned the company for ninety years. A large pair of shears, the last item the Skipper saved as he left his doomed building in 1904, remains one of the family's most treasured heirlooms.

John W. Putts (1851–1910)

Baltimoreans referred to Putts's store at the southwest corner of Charles and Fayette Streets as the "glass palace" because of its large show windows, exclusive clientele, and expensive goods—jewelry, fans, and toilet articles. After it had been reduced to ashes by fire and dynamite explosions, Putts relocated to temporary quarters on Park Avenue near Lexington Street. Impatient with the delays involved in rebuilding the Burnt District, Putts acquired additional property next to his temporary location and built a new glass palace at the northwest corner of Lexington Street and Park Avenue. The new store prospered by selling glassware, china, household furnishings, silverware, leather goods, and jewelry. He also did a brisk business selling restaurant furnishings to hotels, steamboats, and railroad dining cars. John W. Putts died at his home at 2002 Eutaw Place on February 5, 1910, almost the sixth anniversary of the Great Fire.[16]

Mayor E. Clay Timanus (1863–1923)
When Robert M. McLane, a Democrat, died, Timanus, a Republican and president of the city council's Second Branch, succeeded him. Near the conclusion of his service filling McLane's unexpired term, Republicans united behind Timanus as their candidate for mayor after he defeated Frank C. Wachter in the primary election. Timanus lost the bid to succeed himself during the general election when Democrat J. Barry Mahool beat him. Again in 1911, Timanus ran for the office of mayor but he was again defeated, this time by Democrat James H. Preston.[17] Nevertheless, Timanus's achievements as mayor are notable. His contributions to rebuilding and improving Baltimore after the Great Fire were significant.

Governor Edwin Warfield (1848–1920)
Edwin Warfield founded the Fidelity and Deposit, and Fidelity Trust Companies and became president of both. After a stormy administration as Maryland's governor from 1904 until 1908, opponents accused Warfield of heading an ineffective administration. Others later claimed that one could trace many of the good things accomplished once he left office to forces he had set in motion, such as his fight for efficiency and economy in state affairs. As candidate for the Democratic Party's nomination for the United States Senate in 1907, Warfield was defeated in the primary election by ex-Governor John Walker Smith. Warfield, a native of Howard County, spent his later years performing pro bono public service for Maryland.

Four Fatalities
Attributed to the Great Fire★

Private John Undutch
Fell ill on February 16, 1904, while on duty with
Company F, 4th Regiment and died five days later of
pneumonia at his parents' home.[18]

Second Lieutenant John V. Richardson
Fell ill on February 17, 1904, while on duty with
Company E, 4th Regiment. After the National Guard
sent him home with a temperature of 104 degrees,
double pneumonia developed, resulting in his death
a few hours later.[19]

Fireman Mark Kelly
Engineer Mark Kelly of Engine Company No. 16, New
York Fire Department returned home from Baltimore
the night of February 9 and on his arrival at his station
house on East 25th Street became ill. He died on
February 25 at home from pneumonia.[20]

Fireman Lieutenant John A. McKew
Firefighter Lieutenant John A. McKew contracted a
severe cold from exposure during the Great Fire.
Tuberculosis developed, and after a great deal of suffering
he died at age twenty-seven on January 27, 1906, following thirteen faithful years in the service.[21]

★ **Unconfirmed. See pages 104–5**

Firefighting Units that Came to the Aid of Baltimore During the Great Fire, February 7–8, 1904

Maryland

Annapolis
(traveled twenty miles by Annapolis & Baltimore Railroad)
Independent Engine Company No. 2
Water Witch Hook and Ladder Company

Hamilton
(traveled six miles by road)

Havre de Grace
(traveled thirty-six miles via railroad)

Highlandtown
(came two miles by road)
Engine Company No. 2

Relay
(traveled nine miles via B&O Railroad)
Fire Company No. 1 (using hand pumper)

Roland Park
(came four miles by road)
Engine Company No. 1

Sparrows Point
(traveled ten miles by trolley)
Volunteer Fire Company No. 1

St. Denis
(traveled nine miles via B&O Railroad)
No. 2 Reel Company

Westminster
(traveled thirty-six miles by road)

Westport
(came three miles by road)

Washington, DC

(traveled forty miles via B&O Railroad)
Engine Company No. 2
Engine Company No. 3
Engine Company No. 6
Engine Company No. 7
Engine Company No. 8

Of the four major cities that aided Baltimore, Washington's firefighters arrived first. Chief William T. Belt along with Engine Companies No. 3 and No. 6 spearheaded their effort, arriving in Baltimore only one hour and forty-nine minutes after the first alarm.

Pennsylvania

Altoona
(traveled 217 miles via Pennsylvania Railroad)
Altoona Engine Company

Chester
(traveled eighty-four miles via B&O Railroad)
Hanley Engine Company No. 1
Felton Engine Company No. 3

Columbia
(traveled sixty-six miles via railroad)
Columbia Steam Engine & Hose Company No. 1

Harrisburg
(traveled eighty-five miles via Northern Central Railroad)
Hope Engine Company

Hanover
(traveled fifty-six miles via railroad)
Hanover Steam Fire Engine Company No. 1

Philadelphia
(traveled ninety-eight miles via
Pennsylvania Railroad)
Engine Company No. 11
Engine Company No. 16
Engine Company No. 18
Engine Company No. 20
Engine Company No. 21
Engine Company No. 23
Engine Company No. 27
Engine Company No. 43

Phoenixville
(traveled 101 miles via
Pennsylvania Railroad)
Phoenixville Engine Company No. 1

York
(traveled fifty-eight miles via
Northern Central Railroad)
Laurel Engine Company
Vigilant Engine Company

Delaware

Wilmington, DE
(traveled seventy-two miles
via B&O Railroad)
Reliance Engine Company No. 2
Weccacoe Engine Company No. 8
Friendship Engine Company No. 1
Frame Hose Company No. 6

New York City

(traveled 187 miles via Pennsylvania Railroad
& New Jersey Central Railroad)

FIRST CONTINGENT

Engine Company No. 5 stationed at 340
East Fourteenth Street
Engine Company No. 7 from Beekman
Street
Engine Company No. 12 stationed at
261 William Street
Engine Company No. 13 stationed at 99
Wooster Street
Engine Company No. 16 stationed at
223 East Twenty-Fifth Street
Engine Company No. 27 from 173
Franklin Street
Engine Company No. 31 located at
White and Elm Streets

SECOND CONTINGENT

Engine Company No. 26 stationed at
Thirty-Seventh Street between
Seventh and Eighth Avenues
(returned to New York with a dog
named "Baltimore")
Engine Company No. 33 from 42–44
Great Jones Street
Hook and Ladder No. 5 stationed at 96
Charles Street

New Jersey

Atlantic City
(traveled 150 miles via B&O Railroad)

Composite group of volunteer firefighters
including United States Company No. 1,
and Neptune Hose Company No. 1

Trenton
(traveled 135 miles via
Pennsylvania Railroad)
Engine Company No. 1

Virginia

Alexandria
(traveled fifty-one miles via railroad)

Comparison of Major Fires (1871–1906)

Event	DATE(S)	FATALITIES	AREA DESTROYED	COST OF DAMAGE
Chicago Fire[1]	October 8–10, 1871	300	3.3 square miles	$200 million property loss
Iroquois Theater Fire (Chicago)	December 30, 1903	More than 600[2]	Theater only slightly damaged[3]	$50,000 in furnishings & refinishing[3]
Baltimore Fire	February 7–8, 1904	1 reported fatality during the fire and 4 fatalities from illness attributed to the fire[4]	86 blocks[5]	More than $70 million in property losses[5]
San Francisco Earthquake and Fire[6]	April 18–21, 1906	Over 498	490 blocks and portions of 32 others	$350–500 million

1 Paul M. Angle, *The Great Chicago Fire* (Chicago: The Chicago Historical Society, 1971,) p. 1.

2 Nat Brandt, *Chicago Death Trap: The Iroquois Theater Fire of 1903* (Carbondale: Southern Illinois University Press, 2003), dust jacket.

3 H. D. Northrop, *World's Greatest Calamities: The Baltimore Fire and Chicago Theatre Horror* (D. Z. Howell, 1904).

4 Report of Captain W. Guy Townsend, Baltimore Fire Papers, MSA S 956, MdHR 50, 077-1, Maryland State Archives; E. Ridgely Simpson, "At 12 I Covered the Great Baltimore Fire of 1904," *Sunday Sun Magazine*, March 8, 1959; "Baltimore Fire Costs Life: Fireman Kelly of This City With Notable Record Contracted Pneumonia," *New York Times*, February 26, 1904, p. 1; Brennen Jensen, "Lives Lost: One," *The City Paper*, September 13, 2003, p. 18

5 G. W. Horton, *Annual Report of the Chief Engineer for the Baltimore Fire Department*, 1905. Horton's report is a subset to *Twenty-First Annual Report of the Board of Fire Commissioners and Forty-Sixth Annual Report of the Fire Department to the Mayor and City Council of Baltimore for the Fiscal Year Ending December 31, 1904* (Baltimore: Wm. J. C. Dulany Co., City Printers, 1905), pp. 17 & 19.

6 Dan Kurzman, *Disaster!: The Great San Francisco Earthquake and Fire of 1906* (New York: William Morrow, 2001), pp. 248, 251. While the official number of those killed was 498, that seems deliberately miscalculated to indicate that San Francisco is a safe place to work and live, p. 248. Another source estimates that more than 3,000 persons were killed during the San Francisco Earthquake and Fire (Museum of the City of San Francisco, http://www.sfmuseum.net/hist10/06timeline.html).

The Great Battle
Rochester

Notes

Introduction

1 D. J. Cannon, *Heritage of Flames: The Illustrated History of Early American Firefighters* (Pound Ridge, N.Y.: Artisan Books, 1977), 101.

2 Suzanne Ellery Greene Chapelle, *Baltimore: An Illustrated History* (Sun Valley, Calif.: American Historical Press, 2000), 8.

3 Ordinances of the Corporation of the City of Baltimore (passed June 11, 1799). (Baltimore: Printed by Thomas Dobbin at the Telegraph Office), 69–70.

4 Amy S. Greenberg, *Cause for Alarm: The Volunteer Fire Department in the 19th Century City* (Princeton, N.J.: Princeton University Press, 1998), 84–94.

5 Ibid., 165.

6 W. A. Murray, *The Unheralded Heroes of Baltimore's Big Blazes* (Baltimore: E. J. Schmitz & Sons, Inc., 1969), 7.

7 J. Thomas Scharf, *Chronicles of Baltimore* (Baltimore: Turnbull Brothers, 1874), 706.

8 J. A. Cassedy, *The Firemen's Record* (Baltimore: Fireman's Relief Association, 1891), 81–103.

Chapter 1

1 *New York Times*, February 9, 1904.

2 Ibid.

3 J. V. Morris, *Fires and Firefighters* (Boston: Little, Brown, and Co., 1955), 277.

4 W. A. Murray, *Unheralded Heroes*, 43.

5 *Philadelphia Inquirer*, February 8, 1904.

6 Murray, *Unheralded Heroes*, 43.

7 Harold A. Williams, *Baltimore Afire* (Baltimore: Schneidereith & Sons, 1979), 3.

8 Murray, *Unheralded Heroes*, 43; Williams, *Baltimore Afire*, 3.

9 *New York Times*, February 9, 1904.

10 Ibid.

11 "Made Record Run," *Washington Post*, February 8, 1904.

12 *Baltimore Sun*, February 7, 1979.

13 T. King, *Consolidated of Baltimore 1816–1950: A History of Consolidated Gas Electric Light and Power Company of Baltimore* (Baltimore: Baltimore Gas & Electric Co., 1950), 136.

14 *Baltimore Sun*, February 7, 1960.

15 Murray, *Unheralded Heroes,* 48.

16 Ibid.; *New York Times,* February 9, 1904, p. 3.

17 *Baltimore Sun,* February 2, 1975.

18 Ibid., February 7, 1960.

19 Murray, *Unheralded Heroes,* 43.

20 *Baltimore Sun,* February 7, 1960.

21 Williams, *Baltimore Afire,* 12; Murray, *Unheralded Heroes,* 48.

22 Interview with Theodore M. Chandlee Jr., October 11, 2001.

23 King, *Consolidated of Baltimore,* 136–37.

24 Harold A. Williams, *The Baltimore Sun, 1837–1987* (Baltimore: The Johns Hopkins University Press, 1987), 105.

25 *Baltimore Sun,* February 7, 1979.

26 Murray, *Unheralded Heroes,* 46.

27 *Baltimore Sun,* February 7, 1979.

28 Ibid., February 5, 1979.

29 Murray, *Unheralded Heroes,* 46.

30 Williams, *The Baltimore Sun,* 104.

Chapter 2

1 "Made Record Run," *Washington Post,* February 8, 1904.

2 "Ten Thousand at Station," ibid.

3 "Danger in Wires and Falling Wires," ibid.

4 "Mr. Macfarland's Offer of Aid," ibid.

5 "Made Record Run," ibid.

6 "Fireman Reported Killed," ibid.

7 "Our Firemen at Work," ibid., February 9, 1904.

8 Ibid.

9 *Philadelphia Inquirer,* February 8, 1904.

10 Ibid.

11 "Returning Flame-fighters Tell of the Battle to Save Baltimore," ibid., February 10, 1904.

12 Ibid.

13 Ibid., February 9, 1904.

14 *Harrisburg Telegraph,* February 8, 1904.

15 Ibid.

16 *Harrisburg Patriot,* February 9, 1904.

17 *[Harrisburg] Star Independent,* February 8, 1904; *Harrisburg Telegraph,* February 8, 1904.

18 *Harrisburg Telegraph,* February 8, 1904.

19 Ibid.

20 *Harrisburg Patriot,* February 9, 1904.

21 Murray, *Unheralded Heroes,* 46.

22 "Seven New York Engines Ready to Go to Baltimore," *New York Times,* February 8, 1904.

23 "Ovation to New Yorkers," ibid., February 9, 1904.

24 Ibid.

25 "The Fire Laddies Trip to Baltimore," ibid., February 14, 1904.

26 Murray, *Unheralded Heroes,* 46.

27 "Ovation to New Yorkers."

28 "Eye Witnesses Tell of Rush of Flames," *New York Times,* February 9, 1904.

29 "Baltimore's Business Section Totally Destroyed by Fire," *The Afro-American Ledger,* February 16, 1904.

30 Ibid.

31 "New York Firemen Get Warm Welcome," *New York Times*, February 10, 1904.

32 "The Fire Laddies Trip."

33 Ibid.

34 "New York Firemen Get Warm Welcome."

35 "Honors for Baltimore," *New York Times*, February 14, 1904.

36 Ibid.

37 Franklin W. Kemp, *Firefighting by-the-Seashore: A History of the Atlantic City Fire Department, December 3, 1874 – March 1, 1972* (Atlantic City, N.J.: Seashore Fire Buffs, 1972), 219–20.

38 Ibid., 225.

Chapter 3

1 *New York Times*, February 8, 1904.

2 D. K. Yates, *Forged by Fire: Maryland's National Guard at the Great Baltimore Fire of 1904* (Westminster, Md.: Family Line Publications, 1992), 23; *New York Times*, February 8, 1904.

3 Laws of Maryland, 1896, Chapter 89, Article XXXIV.

4 Yates, *Forged by Fire*, 2, 23; *Philadelphia Inquirer*, February 9, 1904.

5 *Baltimore American*, February 17, 1904.

6 Report of Captain Bruce B. Gootee, Baltimore Fire Papers, Maryland State Archives (hereinafter MSA).

7 Yates, *Forged by Fire*, 4.

8 Adjutant General [Baltimore Fire Papers] MSA S 956, MdHR 50, 077-1, MSA.

9 Yates, *Forged by Fire*, 5–6.

10 Ibid., 6; After Action Reports of Hinkley and First Lieutenant W. S. Brownley, Baltimore Fire Papers, MSA.

11 After Action Reports of Captain Lester Kingsbury, Baltimore Fire Papers, MSA.

12 Yates, *Forged by Fire*, 7.

13 *Baltimore American*, February 17, 1904.

14 Yates, *Forged by Fire*, 8.

15 Ibid., 4.

16 *Baltimore Sun*, February 10, 1904; *Annapolis Evening Capital*, February 11, 1904; Yates, *Forged by Fire*, 15.

17 *Philadelphia Inquirer*, February 9, 1904.

18 Yates, *Forged by Fire*, 26; report of Captain Moumonier Rowe, Baltimore Fire Papers.

19 "The Fidelity and Deposit Companies: Celebrating Our Centennial," 1989, 4.

20 Warfield's letter is in the Adjutant General, Miscellaneous Papers, MSA S927, MdHR 50.056-159, MSA; *Report of the Board of Police Commissioners for the City of Baltimore 1904–1905*, 15.

Chapter 4

1 J. W. Clautice, "The Great Fire of February 7, 1904: A News Summary of the Disaster Which Changed the Course of Baltimore's History," *Baltimore*, XLVII, 3 (1954).

2 J. Ryan, "They Never Put Up a Plaque: Tavern Only Link With Outside in 1904 Fire," *Baltimore News-Post*, February 7, 1962.

3 *Baltimore Sun*, February 7, 1979.

4 J. L. Wickes, *Annual Report of the Commissioner of Street Cleaning Fiscal Year Ending December 31, 1904* (Baltimore: Wm. J. C. Dulany Co., 1905), 4.

5 "Boy Got Thrashing for Visiting the Fire," *Baltimore Evening Sun*, February 7, 1979.

6 "The Great Baltimore Fire: A Cigarette and the Wind Destroyed Busy City's Heart," *Baltimore Evening Sun,* February 7, 1979.

7 H. D. Northrop, *World's Great Calamities: The Baltimore Fire and Chicago Theatre Horror . . .* (Philadelphia: National Publishing Co., 1904), 79.

8 Ryan, "They Never Put Up a Plaque."

9 J. A. Miller, *Fares Please!* (New York: Dover Publications, Inc., 1960), 124.

10 "The Great Baltimore Fire: A Cigarette and the Wind."

11 P. Ditzel, *Fireboats: Complete History of the Development of Fireboats in America* (New Albany, Ind.: Fire Buff House Division of Conway Enterprises, Inc., 1989), 26.

12 "Baltimore Fire," *Baltimore Sun,* October 4, 1983.

13 G. W. Horton, *Report of the Chief Engineer* (Baltimore: Wm. J. C. Dulany Co., 1905), 20.

14 "The Great Baltimore Fire: A Cigarette and the Wind."

15 This is not to say it did not happen. The Baltimore waterfront was a haven for sailors, drifters, and recent immigrants. A vanished victim of the fire would not have been the first nameless soul to disappear in Baltimore's murky harbor.

Chapter 5

1 H. L. Mencken, *Newspaper Days, 1899–1906* (New York: Alfred A. Knopf, 1940), 276–77.

2 *New York Times*, February 9, 1904.

3 Williams, *The Baltimore Sun, 1837–1987,* 104.

4 *New York Times,* February 8, 1904.

5 *Philadelphia Inquirer*, February 8, 1904.

6 *Baltimore Herald,* February 8, 1904.

7 Edwin F. Abell died on February 28, 1904, less than three weeks after the fire.

8 *The Baltimore Sun Almanac,* 1905, 80.

9 Gerald W. Johnson et al., *The Sun Papers of Baltimore, 1837–1937* ((New York: Alfred A. Knopf, 1962), 242, 249; Williams, *The Baltimore Sun, 1837–1987,* 101.

10 Williams, *The Baltimore Sun, 1837–1987,* 102.

11 Ibid., 108.

12 *New York Times,* February 9, 1904.

13 Williams, *The Baltimore Sun, 1837–1987,* 108.

14 Johnson et al., *The Sun Papers of Baltimore, 1837–1937* 251

15 Ibid., 252.

Chapter 6

1 *Twentieth Annual Report of the Board of Fire Commissioners to the Mayor and City Council of Baltimore for the Fiscal Year Ending December 31, 1903* (Baltimore, 1904), 5.

2 *Report of the Chief Engineer for the Fiscal Year Ending December 31, 1904* (Baltimore, 1905), 20.

3 Mississippi Wireglass Company, *A Reconnaissance of the Baltimore and Rochester Fire Districts with Some Illustrations and Excerpts from Opinions No Less Authoritative than Significant* (New York: Mississippi Wireglass Co., 1904), 1.

4 *Philadelphia Inquirer*, February 9, 1904.

5 Ibid.

6 Ibid.

7 *New York Times*, February 9, 1904, p. 3.

8 *Philadelphia Inquirer*, February 9, 1904.

9 *Washington Post*, February 8, 1904.

10 *Philadelphia Inquirer*, February 8, 9, 1904.

11 *New York Times*, February 9, 10, 1904.

12 *Philadelphia Inquirer*, February 11, 1904.

13 "Baltimore Quick to Plan Future," *New York Times*, February 11, 1904.

14 On November 2, 1999, voters elected Martin O'Malley Mayor of the City of Baltimore at the age of thirty-six; however, McLane continues to hold the record as the youngest person elected to this office.

15 C. M. Rosen, *The Limits of Power: Great Fires and the Progress of City Growth in America* (New York: Cambridge University Press, 1986), 300.

16 *Wachter v. McLane*, 1903, 2 Baltimore City Reports, 295.

17 Fred Rasmussen, "O'Neill's Sold the Finest Goods in Baltimore," *Baltimore Sun*, January 11, 1998.

18 A. M. Quick, "Water Service at the Baltimore Fire, 1904," paper read at the convention of the American Water Works Association, St. Louis, Mo., June 6–11, 1904, 448–51.

19 Rasmussen, "O'Neill's Sold the Finest Goods in Baltimore."

20 *Baltimore Sun*, April 13, 1969.

21 *Baltimore American*, April 7, 1919; "O'Neill's Sold the Finest Goods in Baltimore."

22 Waverly Press, Inc., *Golden Anniversary 1890–1940* (Baltimore: Waverly Press, 1940), 3–4; E. M. Passano Jr., *Waverly History* (Baltimore: Waverly Press, 1995), 1; Waverly, Inc., *A Century of Progress 1890–1990: Waverly, Inc. Williams & Wilkins Waverly Press* (Baltimore: Waverly Press, 1990), 5. Waverly, Inc., "Edward Boteler Passano August 11, 1872 – June 13, 1946," *The Kalends of the Waverly Press*, 25 (July–August 1946): 4; P. J. Kelly and Peter B. Petersen, "Scientific Management and the Williams & Wilkins Company," *Academy of Management, Management History Division Best Paper Proceedings of the Academy of Management* (August 1992): 150; Peter B. Petersen, "Reflections of Dean Emeritus Robert H. Roy," (1984), 1–2.

23 Waverly, Inc., *A Century of Progress 1890–1990*, 6.

24 Johns Hopkins University, *The Waverly Press: Edward B. Passano's Baltimore Legacy.* Brochure for the Inaugural Exhibit of the Passano Gallery (2002), 1.

25 R. Roy, "Bragolections: The Career Adventures of a Poo-Bah," 1990, unpublished paper describing Rob Roy's days at Waverly Press and in the early history of Waverly Press, 47; Petersen, "Reflections of Dean Emeritus Robert H. Roy," 2.

26 James B. Crooks, *Politics and Progress: The Rise of Urban Progressivism in Baltimore 1895–1911* (Baton Rouge: Louisiana State University Press, 1968), 141.

27 F. P. Steiff, *The Government of a Great City* (Baltimore: H. G. Roebuck & Son, 1935), 8, 9, 12.

28 Rosen, *Limits of Power*, 263.

29 Ibid, p. 296.

30 Harbor Board Annual Reports, 1897–1904. Reports of the City Officers and Departments to the City Council of Baltimore.

31 Detailed presentation of coverage by specific insurance companies is included in Sanborn Map Company Insurance Maps of Baltimore, Maryland (New York, circa 1904). Available in the Maryland Room of the Enoch Pratt Library, Baltimore.

32 Crooks, *Politics and Progress*, 141.

33 Citizen's Emergency Committee Minute Book, February 13–19, 1904, Maryland Historical Society.

34 Ibid.

Epilogue

1 Sherry Olson, *Baltimore: The Building of an American City* (Baltimore: The Johns Hopkins University Press, 1980), 248.

2 B. W. Weaver, "I Remember . . . Baltimore's Thank-You Parade," *Baltimore Sun*, January 5, 1958, 93–94.

3 *Official Program of Maryland Home-Coming Week: Baltimore, October 13 to October 19, 1907*, 1.

4 Robert J. Brugger, *Maryland: A Middle Temperament, 1634–1980* (Baltimore: The Johns Hopkins University Press, 1988), 428.

5 Olson, *Baltimore*, 289.

6 Ibid., 253.

7 Brugger, *Middle Temperament*, 426.

8 Murray, *Unheralded Heroes*, 113.

9 *Baltimore: Its History and Its People*, Vol. III, Biography (New York: Lewis Historical Publishing Co., 1912), 466–67.

10 "Anniversary Today," *Baltimore News-Post*, February 7, 1946; and "Short Story About the Horse," *Baltimore Sun*, March 21, 1954.

11 Williams, *The Baltimore Sun, 1837–1987*, 109.

12 *Baltimore: Its History and Its People*, 3:665–66.

13 Ibid., 3:293–94.

14 W. F. Coyle, *The Mayors of Baltimore*, reprinted from *The Baltimore Municipal Journal* (Baltimore, 1919), 194, 201.

15 Rasmussen, "O'Neill's Sold the Finest Goods in Baltimore."

16 *Baltimore: Its History and Its People*, 3:583–87.

17 W. F. Coyle, *The Baltimore Book*, 5th ed., reprinted from *Baltimore Municipal Journal* (Baltimore, 1916), 205–9.

18 D. K. Yates, *Forged by Fire*, 11.

19 Ibid., 11.

20 *New York Times*, February 26, 1904, 1.

21 Murray, *Unheralded Heroes*, 48.

Index

NOTE: Italicized *page numbers* indicate illustrations or photographs.